EIR (ISSN 0273-6314) *is published weekly
(50 issues), by EIR News Service, Inc.,
P.O. Box 17390, Washington, D.C. 20041-0390.
(703) 777-9451*

European Headquarters: *E.I.R. GmbH, Postfach
Bahnstrasse 9a, D-65205, Wiesbaden, Germany
Tel: 49-611-73650
Homepage: http://www.eirna.com
e-mail: eirna@eirna.com
Director: Georg Neudecker*

Montreal, Canada: 514-461-1557

Denmark: EIR - Danmark, Sankt Knuds Vej 11,
basement left, DK-1903 Frederiksberg, Denmark.
Tel.: +45 35 43 60 40, Fax: +45 35 43 87 57. e-mail:
eirdk@hotmail.com.

Mexico City: EIR, Sor Juana Inés de la Cruz 242-2
Col. Agricultura C.P. 11360
Delegación M. Hidalgo, México D.F.
Tel. (5525) 5318-2301
eirmexico@gmail.com

War with China: Is It Too Late?

If We Don't Match Up to What Obama Is Doing against China, Our Organization Is in Jeopardy

Oct. 29—The real problem is what is seen in Obama's outrageous military provocation against China on Tuesday (Oct 27): Obama is determined to launch a thermonuclear war. Now, what happens to us, if we don't say that and campaign on that? Look at the fraud of Obama's attack against China! Look at his bloody paws! He must be removed! Under the principle of the U.S. Presidency, he can be removed from office,—and if we don't do that, we rapidly get into an ever-more dangerous situation.

You can't fool around and negotiate, or say, "No! I don't believe it!" Don't go around and ask how to do it,—he must be restrained or we're all dead.

We must place this at the top of the list of issues: Don't call it anything else: murder is murder! To say otherwise is a lie. Obama is essentially a murderer, a mass murderer. The President of the United States currently is a mass murderer. If you want to save the United States, you have to say that, or you may be the next one to go. And if you don't use that kind of language, even on the street, you're in trouble. The truth is essential: Obama is a murderer!

Anyone who tries to minimize Obama's war moves against China: tell them they're brain-damaged. People are being murdered by Obama, while you whisper about and pretend not to know.

To the people who whine that "It's not him; it's the system," tell them, "No, it's Obama." If you don't say it's Obama, then you have no right to have any opinion at all. Because if you're condemning people to justify their being murdered, you don't have any rights.

This is murder, plain murder! The evidence is conclusive, and if you don't say it, then what are you? Wishy-washy!

People are afraid that Obama will kill them, too, if he's displeased by them. But the only way to save yourself is: Don't accept that! If you give in, or condone people giving in, you yourself may be writing your own ticket for death. It's gutless wonder time!

To win a war, you must take the enemy down. Obama won't give in unless you take him down. This is an immediate issue now, not ultimately, not over the long term. If you don't have the guts to take that on, then your opinion is worthless. And the inaction of the Congress so far is a condemnation of their morals. They don't understand that they, like every person, will die eventually. Will it be as worthless creatures for mankind,—or as soldiers who know that they're mortal, and are careful how they spend that mortality to rescue mankind? Cowardice is never anything but disgusting.

Obama's mass-murderous wars in the Mideast,—wars based on lies,—have turned the victim countries into Hell on Earth. The situation in Germany is on the edge of an explosion, where despite a continuous tremendous outpouring of agapic help through the innumerable volunteers and aid organizations, yet simply because of the extremely large number of refugees,—tens of thousands per day,—coming to Bavaria from Austria, the limits of capacity are being reached in terms of shelter and personnel. The biggest obstacle to the solution,—a combination of a crash program for public housing construction and a new Marshall Plan for the Middle East and Africa, the extension of the New Silk Road and the World Land-Bridge,—is Schäuble. His insistence on the Black Zero, a balanced budget, is what fuels the xenophobic tendency of parts of the population.

This is triggering a backlash which threatens to break the coalition government. Germany is already cold. It's only a matter of time before some refugee child freezes to death in a makeshift camp. We've presented the case against Obama,—we needn't repeat the evidence again. We have to go for a dramatic effect which will move the audience to change and act.

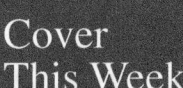

Cover This Week

U.S. Navy

The guided-missile destroyer USS Lassen, which Obama ordered to intrude into Chinese territorial waters on Oct 27 as a war provocation.

Ending Permanent War and Financial Panic: Glass-Steagall And the Global Silk Road

Helga Zepp-LaRouche gave this keynote address to an EIR *Forum at National Press Club in Washington, D.C., on Oct. 27.*

Well, let me welcome all of you. I think most people in the world right now are aware that we are really experiencing a *civilizational* crisis, not only a financial crisis, many military crises around the world, wars, terrorism, hunger, refugees; it's just an enormous number of simultaneous crises. And while all of these individual crises have local causes which trigger them and cause them, I think it's fair to say that the fundamental basis for the strategic civilizational crisis, is the fact that the trans-Atlantic financial system is hopelessly bankrupt. And it is that dynamic which is behind the war danger, which is behind local crises, and is the biggest threat to the world right now.

Because, contrary to what you read in the popular media, the crisis is not solved. As a matter of fact, there have even been warnings in the financial press like *The Economist* and other such magazines, that we could have at *any* moment a repetition of what happened in 2008; that you could have a crash of the financial system of the trans-Atlantic sector, which could be triggered by a whole number of events. For example, if only one of the too-big-to-fail banks went bankrupt, it probably would evaporate the entire trans-Atlantic financial system in a moment.

If that happens, obviously, immediate chaos would break out, because contrary to 2008, there are no more so-called "tools" in the toolbox of the financial institutions. Quantitative easing? It has been done to the hilt. You know, the Bank of Japan, the Federal Reserve, the ECB have had zero interest rate policies for years. Bail-outs have only led to the increase of the debt crisis in all of the trans-Atlantic sector; and bail-in, which is now the law of the land in Dodd-Frank and in the ECB, in the European Union Commission, would only be enough to deal with 1% of the outstanding derivatives debt.

The reason is because the too-big-to-fail banks have increased in size since 2008 by 40-80%, and have outstanding derivative debt contracts of up to $2 quadrillion. And we roughly estimate that if you count all the

UNHCR/M. Henley

A civilizational crisis: Refugees huddled against the cold outside an overcrowded registration center in Hungary close to the Serbian border on Sept. 14.

banking accounts of private people, of businesses, and other financial assets which would go into a bail-in, the total would account for about 1% of that debt. So an instant collapse into chaos is really the danger we are talking about.

Now there is a remedy to that. The remedy is to introduce Glass-Steagall, the banking separation law which was introduced in 1933 by Franklin D. Roosevelt in response to the economic crisis of the early '30s. There are several bills in the U.S. Congress and in the Senate [to do that]—there is actually legislation with the exact same text in the Congress and the Senate. So if the political will could be mobilized, that problem could be solved. But it *has* to be solved. There is no other way but to shut down the casino economy of Wall Street.

Now, as I said, this is just the tip of the iceberg, and the pursuit of the high-risk speculation of Wall Street, of the City of London and of other financial institutions, you know, has led to an unbelievable situation! I think 21% of all people in the United States don't have access to sufficient food; you have about 7% who live in what is defined as extreme poverty; you have 95 million people who are not part of the workforce any more, so you have 104 million eligible Americans who don't have jobs. The poverty rate in Europe, even without the present refugee crisis, one-third of all youth, average, are unemployed! In the south of Europe, over 60% are unemployed.

And if you look at the condition of what is called generally the "Third World," like Africa, I don't know how many hundreds of millions of people have been killed by a policy denying development to that continent and many other nations.

The Refugee Crisis

So now we are hit with an additional problem: the refugee crisis in Europe. I know people in America

UNHCR/M. Henley

A civilizational crisis: Some 2000 refugees trapped at the Serbian-Croatian border, under the glare of border lights.

think this is very far away, but I tell you, this is becoming a key strategic factor which also affects the United States.

It is now publicly debated in Europe that this refugee crisis was caused by U.S. and British wars in the Middle East, by a policy of regime change, by a policy of playing the so-called "Islamic card" going back to Brzezinski in 1975, when he initiated this policy; and then having a policy of always supporting the "good rebels," training them, only to see that the good rebels join the terrorists. Then you have to make a new war against the terrorists, then you have to bet on the "good rebels," and so forth and so on!

This has now led to a situation where basically millions of people are trying to get into Europe. Germany probably will have, at a minimum, one million refugees coming in this year. The UN Human Rights report says that there are presently 60 million people in flight right now. So we're not talking about a temporary refugee crisis. We're talking about a large migration of people running away from war, hunger, epidemics, mainly from Southwest Asia, but also to a certain extent from Africa.

And it is very clear this will not stop! This will not stop, and you see right now the effect: The EU has completely failed. They ignored this problem for many years because they left Italy and Greece completely alone in dealing with it for all these years; there were hundreds of people drowning in the Mediterranean for years! Some of them arrived in Lampedusa in Italy, and the EU said, "That's an Italian problem." The same with Greece.

But now, with the recent developments in Syria, this is really exploding, and you see the pictures. The official figure is that about 3,000 people have drowned in the Mediterranean this year; that's officially, so probably in reality you can say double or many times more. And still people take the risk, knowing there's a 50% chance of not making it. They go and try to get to Europe.

Now the EU has failed again, because just two days ago there was a summit with the Balkan route states, where they then decided to strengthen the outer borders of the EU. The idea of building a "Fortress Europe" is completely ridiculous! That has never functioned and will never function. And then, they said that they want to have certain camps along the Balkan routes; and they said, "Oh, finally, we made the first step to solve the problem."

Now this was after *months* of this crisis going on! And the pictures are horrible! There is no unity in Europe; there is no solidarity; there is no Europe. The EU now turns out to be something which was transformed into an interest group for the banks—namely, the EU after the Maastricht Treaty. You can not pretend to have a "union" which is bound together by nothing other than the defense of the banks and the defense of the high-speculation system. There is no unity because all of the Eastern Europeans are now refusing to take any refugees; you have a situation where the famous "European values,"—where are they? What are we defending against some other cultures when there are no values in Europe?

And of course, Chancellor Merkel did the right thing when she said several weeks ago, "We can manage." It was the right thing to do! Because these refugees have the right for asylum, according to the Geneva Convention, according to the UN Charter; of course, if you stick to the wrong policies, it gets out of hand. And the biggest threat right now, is the maintenance of the present financial policies of Wall Street, the City of London, the ECB, which are reflected by German Finance Minister Wolfgang Schäuble.

Schäuble says we must protect the so-called "black zero," which is a synonym for balanced budgets and zero deficit. This is the idea that no matter how much you must spend for the refugees, the budget must remain balanced, and that means you have to cut in other areas, like social expenditures, kindergarten, schools, and the health system. And naturally, for German people who are in a precarious economic situation already, like the unemployed, like the people who have a low but precarious income, they feel threatened. And therefore, Schäuble's "black zero" fuels the kind of xenophobic reactions which you have heard about: that already this year 500 housing projects for the refugees have been attacked or burned down, and right-wing violence is on the increase.

You see now that President Putin was absolutely correct when he said several months ago, or even a year ago, that the big mistake of the West in supporting Nazis in Ukraine, in the form of the Right Sector, was the danger that this Nazism would spread to other European countries. And you see right now a big increase of conservatives—I'm not saying that all the right-wing governments are Nazis; I'm just saying the current policy increases the right-wing reaction, and it increases some outright fascist elements in many countries in Europe. And this is very, very dangerous.

So the only solution is, obviously, to change the economic policy, to stop what is high-risk speculation for the United States on Wall Street; to stop what is the "black zero" policy of Schäuble in Europe. And, fortunately, there is an alternative.

The Alternative on the Table

Now what's not very well-known—because the Western media in Europe and the United States are generally not reporting it, or if they report it, they misrepresent it—is that there *is* an alternative economic system which has developed. It started really 25 years ago, when we proposed the New Silk Road as a response to the collapse of the Soviet Union; but it was again put energetically on the table by the Chinese government in September 2013, when President Xi Jinping announced in Kazakhstan that China's policy is the creation of a New Silk Road. And in the meantime, this dynamic of building a New Silk Road in the tradition of the ancient Silk Road—meaning an exchange not only of culture, of goods, of ideas, but also of technologies, of improving relations among nations,—this has spread like wildfire!

It spread into the BRICS (Brazil, Russia, India, China, South Africa); the BRICS had a big summit in

Host Photo Agency

An alternative system underway: The BRICS Ministers of Science, Technology, and Innovation meeting on Oct. 28, 2015 in Russia.

Fortaleza, Brazil in July 2014. It was consolidated through another BRICS summit in Ufa, Russia this year; and what you see now is the unfolding of an alternative economic system which is based on completely different principles than the trans-Atlantic high-risk and high-profit speculation.

It is based on real investment in infrastructure, on uplifting populations out of poverty, as China has done in lifting 600 million people out of poverty in the last 30 years; and it is now offering, in reality, the Chinese economic miracle to other countries that participate in the construction of this New Silk Road.

Now this is really taking off. China is building a "Second Panama Canal" in Nicaragua; China is helping to build a transcontinental railway between Brazil and Peru; China is helping to build five canals between Argentina and Chile. And many, many other projects are underway with the high-technology cooperation among many nations, including in nuclear energy and space cooperation, and this process is really an engine of growth. And do not believe all the bad-mouthing claiming that the Chinese economy is collapsing, and that that is the cause of all the problems. It is not true. Although China has a stock market, that does not affect its real economy which is still on a very healthy trajectory.

Now, with this process goes a whole different system of economic and financial institutions, like the

AIIB (Asian Infrastructure Investment Bank), which the United States made a big effort to pressure its allies not to join. Well, what happened? Some 58 or 59 nations immediately joined. The first one, interestingly enough, was Great Britain, because they are a little bit smarter; they know which way the wind is blowing. And then most of the European nations and many Asian nations joined,—and this is now becoming a major institution for the financing of infrastructure in real economy.

But there's also the New Development Bank of the BRICS. Then you have the Shanghai Cooperation Organization Bank; you have the SAARC bank,—that's the bank for the South Asian Association for Regional Cooperation; you have the Silk Road Fund; you have the Maritime Silk Road Fund. So you have the spread of a whole different set of financial institutions which are deliberately set up *not* for speculation, but only for the investment in real industry.

And in a certain sense, that new group of financial institutions is like the lifeboat at the moment when the *Titanic* of the trans-Atlantic system is sinking.

Now, what we have to do,—and there is such a thing as a *Patent rezept*, [German for a patent formula, or a sure remedy] like a *passe-partout* [a masterkey], which really would solve most problems of the world, if we can get the United States to implement Glass-Steagall; shut down Wall Street; then implement a credit system in the tradition of Alexander Hamilton; go back to the traditional American System of economy; and generate large amounts of state credit for production and projects. Then do the same thing in Europe.

The Greek government has insisted for some time that the Greek debt is unpayable, and that there must be a European debt conference in the tradition of the 1953 debt conference, which at that time, cut the German debt by 60%. That deal dealt with the German debt from the period between World War I and World War II, but also the debt from the so-called Marshall Plan. And it is generally acknowledged that the German economic miracle in the post-war period could not have taken place if that debt reduction had not happened.

Therefore, the Greek government's demand for a debt cut is absolutely legitimate, all the more because most of this debt is illegitimate; it was just imposed on the Greek governments only to have 97% of it flow back to the European banks to cover their situation. Three percent of that debt remained in Greece. So, why should the Greek people be continuously tortured into cutting their economy, which has been shrunk by one-third through this austerity policy? No, they have the right to write-off this illegitimate debt.

Now, after such a debt conference in Europe, we could go back to the good policies which helped the German economic miracle in the post-war reconstruction. That is, we would take the equivalent of the *Kreditanstalt für Wiederaufbau*, the Credit Bank for Reconstruction, which was the vehicle for the economic miracle in Germany in the postwar period, and provided state credit in the same way the Reconstruction Finance Corp. of Franklin D. Roosevelt did in the New Deal.

That was the mechanism by which Germany made an economic miracle, and exactly that mechanism should be used today for the financing of pressing physical needs. If you want to solve the refugee problem, we have to provide new credit—and Mr. Schäuble should retire, because he's incompetent and should really not determine where the future of Europe lies. We could issue the credit to build 500,000 public housing units per year for the refugees. Then, we need other investments, like hiring teachers and social workers, and setting up training programs to integrate a lot of these refugees into the construction of their own housing in Europe.

Extend the Silk Road into the Middle East

But this is only one part of the solution. Because the terrorism problem in the Middle East, as important as it is that Putin changed the strategic situation by militarily intervening in Syria,—you know, this problem of terrorism will not be solved by military means alone. Once you defeat terrorism, you need to put in real development.

If you look at Southwest Asia, the entire region is

creative commons

A civilizational crisis: The Iraq National Library and Archive, after being burned and looted in the aftermath of the U.S. invasion in 2003.

desert! From the Atlantic coast of Africa all the way, the Sahel zone, the Sahara, into the Saudi Peninsula, into Southwest Asia, into the Middle East, all the way to China, this is a tremendous belt of desert which is expanding; it's growing. And there is nothing—I mean, look, the Middle East has been bombed back into the Stone Age.

Look at Iraq: Iraq was a functioning country under Saddam Hussein! You may not have liked Saddam Hussein, but it was a functioning country with growing infrastructure, with women having access to universities; the same goes for Qaddafi. You may not have liked Qaddafi, but he developed infrastructure in Africa. Look at Syria. The previous situation in Syria was functioning! You had peace among all religions. You had a secular government which promoted the well-being of its own people, and look at these countries now! They're being destroyed, they're being turned into rubble-fields. And if we want to have a stable future, it is not enough to just reinforce the refugee camps in Turkey, or reinforce the outer borders of Europe as a Fortress Europe.

What I'm saying is that the New Silk Road and the policies adopted by the BRICS countries *are* the solution to these Middle East problems. Because all we have to do is to extend the New Silk Road into Middle East.

Now, people would say, "That would never function. The Middle East has always been the battleground of all these empires, the British, the French, and various others . . . ." But it has reached a point where mankind is faced with the challenge, that either we change the paradigm and establish an order in which all people on this planet can live as human beings, or we will not make it, and we will vanish as the dinosaurs did 65 million years ago because we have proven we are not any smarter.

Now, I think the human species *is* smarter, and therefore, I'm confident that if we put this question on the table and say that if all the major neighbors of Southwest Asia,—Russia, China, India, Iran, Egypt, Italy, Germany, France, and even the United States,—if we all agree and say, "We should develop a Marshall Plan for the Middle East and for Africa. We must now correct the mistakes of not having allowed the development of Africa, of having allowed wars based on lies in the Middle East; and we now unite our efforts and make major reconstruction in the Middle East!"

VOA

A civilizational crisis: The memorial outside the mass shooting at the Sandy Hook Elementary School in December 2012. There has been more than one mass shooting a day in the United States during 2015.

We could declare a war on the desert. We can make new, fresh water; we can desalinate large amounts of ocean water through peaceful nuclear energy. We can use the water in the atmosphere through ionization of moisture, which is being used already in Israel and some Gulf states—we could do that on a large scale; we could have other water projects. We can put in infrastructure. We can build new cities. We can build agriculture and industrialization in both Southwest Asia and Africa, which is eminently possible through the approach we have taken by this report, which says, "The New Silk Road Becomes the World Land-Bridge" by simply extending the existing New Silk Road development into all of these areas.

Now, I think this is eminently possible. I think that all the neighbor countries of the Middle East have a strategic interest, because terrorism and drugs are threatening Russia; Russia has just closed its border with Tajikistan, because they are threatened with terrorism and drugs coming in from Afghanistan and other areas. It's threatening China, because of Xinjiang. India has a big security interest that this problem should be solved, because they have a large Muslim population, and they don't want that Muslim population to be influenced by the radical form of Islam coming from the Wahhabi Salafists.

So there is a common interest naturally in all of Europe, because you know, as much as we welcome,—or at least most of the Europeans or most of the Ger-

mans welcome—the refugees, it is also clear that you cannot deal with hundreds of millions of refugees without the European Union being detonated.

The United States Needs the BRICS!

So, I think we have a unique chance to turn this around. And it would also be in the interest of the United States.

The United States right now insists that there should be a unipolar world order. President Obama has just reiterated that in his speech to the United Nations, by saying that the United States has the largest military ever in history; and just today we got news that the Administration has sent the *USS Lassen* guided missile destroyer to the South China Sea, which has drawn a big protest from China. The Obama Administration just announced that they will put troops on the ground in Syria, which from a standpoint of international law is problematic, because they have not been invited to do so; so right now, the United States has chosen another course.

But the United States would benefit by joining with the BRICS, by joining with the New Silk Road in development! In bringing peace to the Middle East, in building up other countries of the world. But it would not only mean that the United States would join development projects in Southwest Asia and other areas of the world; the United States urgently needs development itself. The U.S. economy is collapsed; you have poverty, you have an unbelievable social situation! I mean the killings, police killings of black people, black-on-black killing, the school shootings—it's a collapse! It's a civilizational crisis here in the United States!

There is no fast train! Have you ever travelled one mile on a fast train in the United States? [laughter] Definitely not: You have to go to China to enjoy travelling for 18,000 km by fast train, which has the finest fast train I have ever travelled on: They're smooth, they're steady, they don't shake like European fast trains. So it's a pleasure.

The United States *urgently* needs improvement of its highways, without potholes into which you can vanish with your car,—which is a hazard to your life every time you travel these roads! So, if the United States would say, we'll go back to an FDR policy, and rebuild our economy, have collaboration not only to build a fast train from Los Angeles to Las Vegas, but to build a real system, a transcontinental railway system with high-speed trains; build new highways; fight the desert in Texas and in California; build some new cities,—the United States could *easily* transform

its military apparatus to produce useful, productive things.

Now, I think the whole world is waiting for that, and what we are trying to do, is we are trying to cause this shift to happen, because it *is* an American tradition. It was the tradition of Benjamin Franklin, of George Washington, of John Quincy Adams, of Abraham Lincoln, Alexander Hamilton, Franklin D. Roosevelt, and John F. Kennedy, so it is not impossible. We just have to evoke the better tradition of America to make that happen.

So that is where I think we are. I think we are really in danger if a collapse of the system happens without the reform of Glass-Steagall to protect the normal population from that; we could really end up in mass killings of an unprecedented dimension. I mean, if this happens in Europe on top of the refugee crisis, I think we would have civil war in Europe, and we probably would have civil war in the United States.

So I think the incentive to change policy while there is still time, is gigantic. And the optimistic note is that the alternative is already in place. Thank you. [applause]

Senator Mike Gravel Returns to Washington, Joins With LaRouche

by Mike Billington

Nov. 1—The National Press Club in Washington, D.C., was the scene on Tuesday, Oct 27, of a forum sponsored by *Executive Intelligence Review* (*EIR*),—this magazine,—featuring Schiller Institute founder Helga Zepp-LaRouche and former U.S. Senator Mike Gravel. Its title was "Ending Permanent Warfare and Financial Panic—Glass Steagall and the New Global Silk Road."

The collaboration of Sen. Gravel with Helga and Lyndon LaRouche, represents a significant step towards the absolutely necessary creation of a team of political and scientific leaders in the United States to end the immediate danger of thermonuclear war under the Presidency of the crazed killer Barack Obama. It must function as a "Presidential committee," capable of formulating the required economic and strategic policies for the next U.S. President.

While Helga Zepp-LaRouche is well-known (and her presentation at the Washington *EIR* Forum is transcribed in this issue of *EIR*), Sen. Mike Gravel, who served in the U.S. Senate from 1969-1981, representing the State of Alaska, is far less well known to Americans today. This is because his many acts of political courage won him the hatred of Wall Street and the leading political and media institutions under Wall Street's domination. This report aims to correct that problem, and in the process shed light on crucial aspects of modern U.S. history which are of great importance today.

The Pentagon Papers

Sen. Gravel is best known and remembered,—despite the subsequent efforts of the press to make him a "non-person,"—as the U.S. Senator who read the "Pentagon Papers" into the *Congressional Record* in 1971. By thus circumventing President Nixon's frantic efforts

The EIR *forum at the National Press Club October 27. From left to right: Mike Billington of* EIR, *Helga Zepp-LaRouche, and Senator Mike Gravel.*

to cover up his crimes in Vietnam (and those of the Lyndon Johnson Administration before him), Sen. Gravel helped to force Nixon's later resignation. And by exposing the fact that the U.S. was losing, not winning, that war, Senator Gravel helped to end it.

It is a dramatic story, powerfully told in Sen. Gravel's autobiography, *A Political Odyssey: The Rise of American Militarism and One Man's Fight to Stop It,* by Sen. Gravel and Joe Lauria (Seven Stories Press, 2011).

Daniel Ellsberg was a former Defense Department analyst who was a member of a team at the RAND Corporation working on a "Top Secret-Sensitive" analysis on behalf of Secretary of Defense Robert McNamara (one of the criminals responsible for the mass murders of the Indochina Wars). Ellsberg decided in 1971 that he was morally required to leak the entire 7,100 page study, to expose and stop the crimes against the U.S. Constitution and against humanity being perpetrated in the U.S. war on Indochina.

The study covered the role of the United States, France, and others in Vietnam going back to the 1940s; the British sabotage of Franklin Roosevelt's effort to prevent the return of the colonial powers to their colonies after World War II; and President Truman's complicity with the British and other European imperial powers in re-establishing their colonies. It detailed what were unquestionably war crimes by the United States under Presidents Johnson and Nixon, while demonstrating that both administrations had massively lied to the American people in order to cover up those war crimes.

Ellsberg gave these so-called "Pentagon Papers" to the *New York Times*, the *Washington Post*, and several other leading newspapers, which began publishing them in segments. But President Nixon imposed injunctions on the newspapers, halting publication. Ellsberg then went to several members of Congress, proposing that they make the document public by reading it into the *Congressional Record*. He told them they could rely on the "Speech or Debate" clause of the Constitution, which holds that a Member of Congress "shall not be questioned in any other place" on anything said in the confines of the Congress, excepting only "treason, felony or breach of the peace."

Several Congressmen who agreed with Ellsberg that the papers ought to be released, and also agreed that they were legally permitted to do so, nonetheless

U.S. Senate Historical Office

Senator Mike Gravel in 1973, soon after winning his Supreme Court case on his release of the Pentagon Papers in Congress.

refused. They placed their careers, or their fears of ostracism, ahead of their moral and patriotic responsibility. At just that moment, Sen. Mike Gravel was holding a one-man filibuster against the draft, which was sending young men to die in Vietnam for no higher purpose. He readily agreed to read the document into the *Congressional Record*.

In his *Foreword* to Sen. Gravel's book, Ellsberg wrote: "Mike Gravel lived up to my initial impression of him as perhaps the only member of the Senate who took his oath to the Constitution more seriously than his political standing in the club. He also had the guts to infuriate an administration by exposing its guilty secrets."

Sen. Gravel called a hearing of the subcommittee he headed, Buildings and Grounds, read aloud the opening pages of the Pentagon Papers, and then submitted the entire document into the record. He openly sobbed while reading the documents aloud, as the memory welled up in his mind of the maimed and battered U.S. soldiers that he had visited just days earlier at Walter Reed Army Hospital.

The 2008 Campaign

Years later, in 2007, the government had once again been firmly taken over by the war party through Bush and Cheney, while the leading Democratic candidates for President were equally committed to the "perpetual war" policy launched by Bush under the guise of the "war on terrorism." Sen. Gravel determined that he had no choice but to run for President.

In a Democratic Presidential debate on July 23, 2007, with Hillary Clinton, Barack Obama, and the other candidates on the stage, Sen. Gravel demanded that the United States simply get out of Iraq immediately. He said: "Our soldiers died in Vietnam in vain. You can go to Hanoi now and buy a Baskin-Robbins ice cream cone; we have given them most-favored-nation trade status. What did all these people die for? What are they dying for right now in Iraq, every single day? Let me tell you, there's only one thing worse than a soldier dying in vain. It's more soldiers dying in vain."

The moderator immediately turned to candidate Barack Obama to ask him if he agreed that those soldiers were dying in vain. Obama said that the troops had done everything they had been asked to do,—which is to say "my country right or wrong," a concept Sen. Gravel denounced in his Press Club speech this Oct. 27. "Well for me, that's the most immoral statement you can make," he said. "If you love your country, and you see it doing something wrong, you should do something to correct it. And that's where I have charted my course in life."

The 28 Pages

Sen. Gravel was taken to court by the Nixon Administration, which used a technicality to attempt an end-run around the "speech or debate" clause. Sen. Gravel won that case, right up to the Supreme Court. That 1972 decision, *Gravel v. U.S.*, carries momentous implications for one of the most pressing issues of our own day,—the "secret" classification by George W. Bush and Barack Obama of the chapter in the Joint Congressional Report on 9/11, which concerns the funding of the 9/11 hijackers.

When Obama ran for the Presidency, he promised the families of the 9/11 victims that he would release that 28-page chapter, which is well-known (despite being classified), to expose the role of the Saudi monarchy, and especially the then-Saudi Ambassador to the United States, Prince Bandar (a bosom buddy of the Bush family). The Saudis funnelled funds to the key hijackers, both through state "charities" and directly from Bandar and his family. A huge fight to force release of those 28 pages is being waged by the 9/11 families, the LaRouche organization, several members of Congress, and others. There are court cases, there bills in both Houses of Congress, and groups are mobilizing the citizenry.

While visiting Washington for the *EIR* Forum, Sen. Gravel also met with several current and former Senators and their aides. He delivered a simple message: Any one of you, he said, if you had the courage, could do exactly what I did. Simply take the 28 pages to the floor of the Congress, and read them to the American people. What would be exposed would not simply be the true history of that evil event, but also the fact that ever since Sept. 11, 2001, the Presidents of the United States, both Bush and Obama, have been in collaboration with the very institutions still actively funding and arming the terrorists internationally,—the Wahhabi clerics and monarchs of Saudi Arabia.

A recent scholarly article prepared for publication in a law review and given to Sen. Gravel by its authors, argues persuasively that the Supreme Court decision in *Gravel v. U.S.* makes clear that, were a member of Congress, or a group of members, to read the 28 pages into the Congressional record, they would be totally immune from any legal actions against them. The article also notes that the Senate and the House would not be permitted to take action against that member or members either.

Since both houses have in fact called on the Executive Branch to release the 28 pages, to release them in this way would not contravene the will of the Congress. The article goes on to show that the Joint Congressional 9/11 Investigation is the property of the Congress, not the Executive branch, which therefore has no constitutional right to classify it. In fact, the Constitution *requires* the Congress to publicly disclose Congressional proceedings, whenever the Congress itself has not ruled that secrecy is needed.

The issue, then, is purely one of the courage by the members of Congress, to do what is both legal and morally compelling. Only fear is holding back immediate declassification of the 28 pages, with their implied criminal indictment of Obama.

It was George W. Bush who first classified the 28 pages, to cover up his perpetual war campaign and terrorist drone-assassinations. But as Sen. Gravel told his Washington, D.C. audience on Oct. 27, "The difference between Bush and Obama is zero." He characterized the policy of both the Bush and Obama administrations in the Middle East as that of the Four Horsemen of the Apocalypse,—Conquest, War, Famine and Death: "That's our foreign policy! You can call it 'Obama has the Four Horsemen of the Apocalypse, and he's riding it like a chariot.' When you really look at it in depth, it just breaks your heart. As Helga just outlined, it's so easy to pursue the other course; it's so much more humane to pursue the other course."

In his 2007 Presidential campaign, Sen. Gravel grew tired of hearing Obama and Hillary Clinton (among others) claim to oppose Bush's war on Iraq, while refusing to demand an immediate end to that war and other illegal wars. At the same time, they threatened that "all options are on the table" in dealing with Iran and other nations on the U.S. hit-list.

In the April 26, 2007 Democratic Presidential debate in Orangeburg, S.C., Sen. Gravel was asked, "Who are the three most important enemies of the United States?" He replied, "We have no important enemies. What we need to do is to begin to deal with the rest of the world as equals. And we don't do that. We spend more as a nation on defense than all the rest of the world put together. Who are we afraid of? Iraq has never been a threat to us. We invaded them. I mean, it is unbelievable. The military-industrial complex not only controls our government, lock, stock and barrel, but they command our culture.... With respect to Iran, we've sanctioned them for 26 years. We scared the bejesus out of them when the President said 'They are evil.'... Who in the hell are we going to nuke? Tell me, Barack. Barack, who do you want to nuke?"

After the debate, Obama came over to him and said, "Who the Hell are you, Gravel, to question my morality?" Sen. Gravel notes: "I challenged his morality then, and I've been proven right today."

The Alaska Pipeline

Sen. Gravel refers to himself as an "environmental growther." By that he means that he understands that it is the scientific and technological advancement of the

creative commons/Criag Michaud

Mike Gravel in Manchester, New Hampshire, two days before the January 8, 2008 Democratic primary.

economies of all nations, which is the only guarantee of peace and prosperity for mankind,—and only such advancement allows us maintain the environment.

As Senator from Alaska, he fought for and won the fight to build the Alaska Pipeline,—a miracle of construction which has been of benefit for the nation as a whole. It was nearly defeated by the then-emerging "environmentalist" movement, with help from Sen. Scoop Jackson of the State of Washington, the father of the neocons. Jackson tried his best to subvert the project, but he was defeated by Sen. Gravel by one vote in the Senate. However, soon after that legislative victory, the anti-growth fanatics succeeded in locking up huge portions of Alaska from development, despite fierce resistance from Sen. Gravel.

In the Oct. 27 forum in Washington, D.C., he said, "I've been involved in many battles in this regard. There are two elements of environmentalists. There are the 'preservationists.' These are the people who want to put on a loin cloth and go back and live in a cave. The real environmentalists understand that we have localized problems, and that science and technology can help us get out of these problems. The answer is not to limit human growth, but to be sure that that growth is fair and proper and healthy for human beings."

Stopping the U.S. Military Re-Colonization of the Philippines

Sen. Gravel's character was on display this year when he learned that Obama was planning to militarily re-occupy the Philippines. In the 1990s, the Philippines had unceremoniously thrown the United States out of its military bases there, and added a new clause to their Constitution forbidding any foreign military bases on Philippine territory. To circumvent the Philippine Constitution, Obama and his subservient President of the Philippines, Noynoy Aquino, connived to sign an "Enhanced Defense Cooperation Agreement" (EDCA) which invited the United States to establish facilities for their most advanced air, land, and sea weaponry and

U.S. Marines arrive at the Villamor Air Base, Philippines, on Nov. 10, 2013.

personnel within the Philippines, but all within Philippine military bases. EDCA pretends that these will not be "foreign bases" but only "guests" of the Philippines!

Of course, the over-riding real-world issue, is that the criminal Obama is trying to establish these Philippine military bases to prepare for war with China.

Now, EDCA is being contested in the Philippine Supreme Court, on the obvious legal grounds that it breaches the nation's Constitution. On learning of the case, Sen. Gravel took it upon himself to prepare a Friend of the Court brief (called a "Petition for Intervention" in the Philippines), calling on the Supreme Court to reject the agreement on both legal and moral grounds.

Sen. Gravel's brief quotes the former Chairman of the U.S. Joint Chiefs of Staff Gen. Martin Dempsey, who warned the U.S. government against the "Thucydides Trap,—where Athenian fear of a rising Sparta made the Peloponnesian War inevitable." He argues that "China's ascendancy is primarily economic in nature, and no evidence suggests that it seeks global military hegemony, even though its economic interests are global." He calls on the Philippines to "safeguard its own sovereign interests, while avoiding military engagements and a possible war that no one wants."

Sen. Gravel states that he is taking this action because "I love my country. However, I hold my love of mankind above that of my country. I hold the life of any human equal to that of any American."

He goes beyond the current crisis of the Obama war threats against Russia and China, tracing the history of America's descent into a European-modeled colonial policy as beginning with the Spanish-American war. At that time, the United States "purchased" the Philippines from Spain, even after having defeated the Spanish there. Rather than establishing the independence of the nation thus freed from colonialism, the United States maintained its rule. It carried out a bloody suppression of the Philippine independence forces (which had been fighting the Spanish before the Americans arrived), and established America's first colony. Only in the 1930s, with the election of Franklin Roosevelt, was that atrocity partially overturned,—but not completely, due to Roosevelt's early death.

Sen. Gravel warns that the return of U.S. military forces to the Philippines would make it a battleground for an American war on China. Once again it will be the "whorehouse for the U.S. military," as it was during Vietnam. He points to China's astonishing economic growth, lifting 600 million citizens out of poverty in a mere 30 years, and to the "New Maritime Silk Road" and the new international banking institutions created by China and their partners in the BRICS nations.

He writes in the brief: "Compare China's vision for a successful, prosperous, economically unified world to what America offers by way of a militarized world that brooks no challenge to its hegemonic leadership. Compare the suffering of untold numbers of people in a plethora of nations around the world over the last 30 years, a suffering inflicted by the hubris of backroom American neocons punishing people with economic sanctions to bring about regime change, and their liberal interventionists wantonly invading sovereign nations that do not conform to their ideological standards."

Sen. Gravel recognizes the difficulties caused by the conflicting claims over the islands of the South China Sea and the East China Sea, but offers a possible solution. Chinese President Xi Jinping, he says, should call on the UN to sponsor a meeting of the countries surrounding the South China Sea and the East China Sea,—and only those countries,—with the idea of addressing these seas as a "Commons." That is, an area where sovereignty claims are temporarily put aside in favor of joint development of the region and the of natural resources under the Sea. In fact, China's recent development of several artificial islands in the region is intended, according to their Foreign Ministry, for every nation's use, not just for China.

An artist's sketch of the proposed Bering Strait Railway Tunnel between Alaska and Russia, commissioned by Cooper Consulting Co. for Alaska Governor Frank Murkowski.

Obama ordered a U.S. warship to breach the 12-mile territorial limit of one of China's newly-created islands on the very day of the *EIR* forum in Washington, Oct. 27. Sen. Gravel describes the U.S. claim that they are militarily challenging China's sovereignty in the South China Sea in order to defend the "freedom of navigation," as "disingenuous," especially in light of the U.S. refusal to ratify the UN Convention on the Law of the Sea (UNCLOS), which Sen. Gravel fought for as a Senator.

He concludes his brief to the Philippine Supreme Court with two sub-sections, one titled "Save Yourselves," and the other "Save Us from Ourselves."

Sen. Gravel and the LaRouche Movement

Although Sen. Gravel was in touch with the LaRouche movement several years ago, he was recently drawn to work more closely with LaRouche in response to the *EIR* report prepared in 2014, titled **The New Silk Road Becomes the World Land-Bridge.** (See www. worldlandbridge.com) Having represented Alaska, he was particularly drawn to the idea of Russian-U.S. cooperation in building a tunnel under the Bering Strait, an idea Lyndon LaRouche has long advocated, as has Russian President Vladimir Putin. The long-projected Bering Strait Tunnel project, linking the United States and Russia directly by rail, will further "war-avoidance"

through joint infrastructure policies which address the common interests of both nations and the world.

At a Schiller Institute forum in Manhattan on Sept. 12, 2015, Sen. Gravel said: "The Global Land-Bridge report offers a bold vision of how science, progress and infrastructure-led development initiatives are connecting the planet in new ways, and may prove to be an antidote to many of the retrograde ideologies and stalled political systems that have emerged in recent years. The report is also innovative in that it returns the focus of geopolitics to the Eurasian landmass, suggesting that new, rising powers may become more influential than commonly anticipated, including countries like India and Brazil. It is a valuable read for American strategists, who can take this report's thesis as a reminder that engaging the world, especially in Africa and Central Asia, and contributing the best of America's tradition of innovation, is a key way to keep America as a global leader."

At the Oct. 27 *EIR* Forum in Washington, D.C., Gravel concluded his presentation: "So, let me rest on that, and just say that I'm delighted to be associated with the LaRouche organization and the wisdom they've brought forward in their leadership role. And here, I'm taking a page out of their book, suggesting that the leadership of China should take the initiative and bring the Silk Road to the commons of the South China Sea."

The New Silk Road in the Middle East and Africa Must Become A Noah's Ark for the Refugees!

by Helga Zepp-LaRouche, Chair of the German Civil Right Movement Solidarity political party (BüSo)

Oct. 31—The political temperature in Germany is reaching the boiling point. As conservative and right-wing layers irresponsibly spread scare stories combining real but solvable problems with visions of horror, the opposition to Chancellor Merkel is growing. A phalanx has formed ranging from Christian Social Union (CSU) chairman Horst Seehofer (CSU is the sister party of Merkel's CDU), who issued an ultimatum in the hopes of forcing through a change in Merkel's refugee policy, to a growing opposition within Merkel's own Christian Democratic Union (CDU), which intends to impose Wolfgang Schäuble as the successor to Chancellor Merkel.

If that happens, Germany's future might as well be buried. All of Schäuble's policy proposals—be it concerning Greece or the refugees, from Brüning-style austerity to the "Black Zero" (zero deficit) budget policy—exclusively serve the interests of the banks and speculators, to the detriment of the people and the common good. The view of these ideologues, that the hopelessly bankrupt trans-Atlantic financial system can be saved by brutal budget cuts and a Fortress Europe defended by a new Limes wall, are about as sustainable as East German communist leader Erich Honecker's statement of Aug. 14, 1989: "Nothing, neither an ox nor an ass can stop the progress of socialism." Of course, three months later, Honecker was history.

Failures to Act

Willi Wimmer (CDU), a former Secretary of State in the Ministry of Defense, has one thing right, when he insists that if Merkel and others keep emphasizing that we have to fight the root causes of the refugee crisis, then

we would have to ban German airspace for the American drone murderers. Because that is the cause of it.... These are NATO refugees, so we need to be clear about that. If we reduce the world around us to rubble, we will not remain unscathed.

Wimmer often says correct things, but why then, for

Bundesregierung/Kugler

German Chancellor Angela Merkel at a press conference after a European Commission meeting on the refugee crisis.

heaven's sake, does he look to Schäuble as the only viable alternative to Merkel? You might just as well appoint a Bush as the proconsul for Germany!

Regarding the refugee crisis, Wimmer speaks of negligence on the part of the State, because this problem did not fall from the sky. Absolutely! There is even a long series of State failures to act that led to the current situation, and it is high time to name them openly and then to correct them.

The long series of wars in Southwest Asia and Africa are responsible for the current refugee crisis, built one and all upon lies and as a result of the neo-con doctrine, the "Project for a New American Century" (PNAC). What is and was behind that, is the idea of building a unipolar world after the end of the Soviet Union, and toppling any government that stands in the way of that idea through regime change. For that, Islamic extremists have continually been used, from the mujahideen in Afghanistan in the 1980s to al-Qaeda, Jabhat al-Nusra, and ISIS, as well as their various offshoots.

And as long as the German government provides arms to Saudi Arabia or Qatar, while these governments finance the Wahhabite Salafism that is behind ISIS, and as long as the Ramstein airbase is tolerated as a hub for drone operations, the State will continue to be derelict. One correction of this shortcoming would be to abrogate the contracts for the Ramstein, Stuttgart, and other bases that are involved in the drone war, and to call on the U.S. Administration to share the costs of dealing with the the refugees.

Another obvious example of negligence by the State is the years-long indifference toward the situation in Lampedusa, Italy, as well as other "detention centers" in Greece, Malta, Spain, and previously in Libya. For years, refugees have been drowning as they try to flee across the Mediterranean, which was increasingly turned into a giant lake of the dead. Do the Schäubles,

UNHCR/I. Prickett

One of countless refugees from Syria. This woman had collapsed from seasickness and fatigue after the journey from Turkey to the island of Lesbos.

Draghis, Lagardes, and Bernankes of this world really believe that a large part of the world can actually be cut off from economic development for decades—or actually, for centuries under colonialism—by "conditionalities," and that the resulting system of unimaginable injustice in the world, in which 80 individuals possess as much wealth as half of humanity, can continue to exist over the long term?

The current refugee crisis has been in the making for a long time, and will escalate further, as long as the injustice in the current world order that cries out to Heaven is not eliminated.

The blatant failure of the EU in this situation is no surprise. Since the Maastricht Treaty that created the EU in 1992, the bloated bureaucracy in Brussels has turned into a mega-lobby for the financial oligarchy, and its complete lack of "European values" is now trumpeted throughout the world in cacophony. The entire concept of the Frontex border-control organization, whose primary task is to scare off and push back the refugees, is an open indictment of the EU's inhumanity. *Die Welt* reported on the unspeakable behavior of the Frontex staff on the Greek islands—almost all of them from Eastern European countries, which refuse to admit a single refugee—, who watched the people who were fighting for their lives through binoculars, without lifting a finger.

The Chinese Offer

There is only one way to overcome the refugee crisis: A real development perspective for Southwest Asia and Africa must be immediately placed on the agenda, as we have proposed in our study "The New Silk Road Becomes the World Land-Bridge." The potential for this already exists through China's policy for development of the New Silk Road, also called "One Belt, One Road." Chancellor Merkel, in her recent trip to China, asked Chinese Prime Minister Li Keqiang for help in coping with the refugee crisis, and he assured her that China will help to stabilize the countries from which the refugees come.

At the just-ended Syria Conference in Vienna, which brought together for the first time Russia, the United States, Turkey, Iran, Saudi Arabia, the United Kingdom, France, Germany, and the UN, China was also represented. Chinese Deputy Foreign Minister Li Baodong presented a four-part initiative to help solve the crisis in Syria politically. The UN, he said, should have the lead role in mediating among the different groups, and—this is the most important—the reconstruction process in Syria should start immediately, so that the warring parties can see the peace dividend that awaits them as soon as the war ends.

Precisely that is the main idea of extending the New Silk Road to the Middle East and Africa: that is, to create an irresistible incentive so that people see hope for the future in their homeland.

At the opening of the recent "Silk Road Forum 2015" in Madrid, Li Wei, the Director of the Development Research Center (DRC) of the Chinese State Council, presented the wonderful idea that the nations of the world could build "an immense and open Noah's Ark" around the Chinese Silk Road program, which would provide a way out of the financial crisis and bring stability and recovery for the global economy. Li Wei described the Silk Road Economic Belt and the Maritime Silk Road as the way to overcome structural contradictions and to usher in the next phase of global prosperity. Through such cooperation with other nations, the nations could also solve their own domestic contradictions.

Spanish Deputy Trade Minister Jaime García-Legaz

Xinhua/Xie Haining

The Director of the Development Research Center of the State Council Li Wei opening the Silk Road Forum on Oct. 28 in Madrid.

stressed that the best phase of Spanish-Chinese cooperation still lies ahead. This was also the tenor at the recent State visit by President Xi Jinping to the United Kingdom, where effusive speeches were given about the coming Sino-British golden age.

But the most important partner in Europe remains Germany, of course, whose capacities in high technology and especially its *Mittelstand* [small and medium-sized industrial enterprises] best meet the requirements of the Chinese goal of doubling the standard of living by 2025.

The opportunity lies before us to not only overcome the refugee crisis and to create a Noah's Ark with the help of the New Silk Road program for all people and nations in need, but also to achieve a completely new form of cooperation among nations, for the common aims of mankind. We only need to seize it, and every one of you reading these lines is called upon to participate in bringing it about.

The historical moment has arrived at which we can achieve a truly human world order, and we dare not let it pass us by!

This article, which appeared first in the weekly Neue Solidarität, *was translated from German.*

The British Empire's Campaign To Subvert China's Confucian Revival

by Mike Billington

Oct. 28—China today, under its dynamic leader President Xi Jinping, has renewed the ancient philosophic and moral outlook of Confucianism, based on the concepts of harmonious relations within society and between nations, through fostering creativity and discovery,—both in the Chinese citizenry and the world's population. This tradition was demonized during the dark days of the 1966-76 Cultural Revolution, when Western science and culture were denounced along with China's own Confucian culture. Today, China's incredible transformation over the past 30 years,—lifting 600 million people out of poverty and extending its economic miracle to the world through the New Silk Road Economic Belt and the New Maritime Silk Road,—has infuriated the imperial lords of the City of London and Wall Street, which are careening into financial collapse. London's puppet Barack Obama is waging perpetual warfare around the world, to disrupt the new paradigm centered on China and its BRICS partners.

In addition to military threats against China, the British have launched a campaign to subvert the philosophic and cultural foundation of China's rise to prosperity and world leadership. It is not an entirely new policy—it dates back to the very earliest days of British colonization in areas of China—but it has a great urgency in British eyes, since China's rise is seen, correctly, as a major contributor to the final demise of Empire. Thus, they believe, the Confucian revival must be destroyed, and what must be destroyed must first be subverted.

Prince Philip's Campaign against Confucianism

In the late summer of 2013, in Dengfeng, China, the Queen's con-

sort Prince Philip, together with his Daoist religious advisor Martin Palmer and the self-proclaimed "New Confucian" scholar from Harvard, Tu Wei Ming, launched a program designed to subvert China's astonishing pace of development, undermine President Xi Jinping's "One-Belt, One-Road" New Silk Road initiative, and move towards realizing Prince Philip's goal of reducing the world's population to about one billion people. The primary vehicle for this demonic project is called the International Confucian Ecological Alliance (ICEA). Its intent is to falsely portray Confucianism as a green cult opposed to the rapid pace of development that has transformed China over the past three decades into a leading force for peace and development in the world.

To understand the intention of the ICEA, first consider the following. Prince Philip has spent his entire life dedicated to population reduction. He told *People Magazine* in 1981: "Human population growth is prob-

www.iceaworld.org

The founding conference of the International Confucian Ecological Alliance, held in Dengfeng, China in 2013. Martin Palmer is seated 5th from the right.

ably the single most serious long-term threat to survival. We're in for a major disaster if it isn't curbed.... If it isn't controlled voluntarily, it will be controlled involuntarily by an increase in disease, starvation and war." He is most famous for expressing his wish to be reincarnated as "a deadly virus, in order to contribute something to solve overpopulation."

Philip's other major accomplishment was the promotion of the World Wildlife Fund (WWF), the leading environmentalist movement in the world, first as President of the WWF-UK (1961-1982), and then International President (1981-1996). He worked together with Nazi Party member Prince Bernhard of Holland, and British ideologue Sir Julian Huxley. Huxley, in his 1962 essay "Too Many People," argued that overpopulation was a graver danger than nuclear war, and "a problem so serious as to override all other world problems, such as soil erosion, poverty, malnutrition, raw material shortages, illiteracy, and disarmament."

Secondly, consider that China is not only the world's largest nation by population, with nearly 1.4 billion people, but is also the world's fastest growing nation economically, having lifted over 600 million people out of poverty in the short span of 30 years. To the British Empire, China's "threat" is to take this process of rapid industrial development to the rest of the world, especially to the former European colonies in Africa, South America, and Asia, which have remained underdeveloped due to the neo-colonial conditions imposed upon them by their former colonial masters and those masters' international financial institutions.

Thus, British Royal Family asset Barack Obama told South African college students in 2013 (drawing on the fraudulent "global warming" scare), that if all the African youth aspire to "raise living standards to the point where everybody's got a car, and everybody's got an air conditioner, and everybody's got a big house,—the planet will boil over."

Thus, the Empire is hastening to break China, to subvert the optimism of the Chinese people under Xi Jinping's "win-win" projects to bring the Chinese miracle to all of Asia, Africa and South America. This December's COP21 "Global Warming" conference in Paris, is intended to impose mandatory CO_2 emission limits on all of the world's nations, an insane policy based on the scientifically fraudulent claim that CO_2

youtube

Prince Philip's man Martin Palmer at the World Wildlife Fund's 2011 Fuller Science Symposium. He embraces the Daoist adage: "We should cultivate the way of no-action and let nature be itself."

causes global warming. The global warming scare is a hoax formulated by the same British Empire which intends to use this fraud to impose its actual policy intention,—to reduce the world's population through economic deprivation and war.

In the Global Warming conference held in Copenhagen in 2009 (COP15), China and India successfully blocked the Empire's intended genocide by refusing to accept such limits on CO_2 emissions. As Indian President Narendra Modi told UN Secretary General Ban Ki Moon this year, India will not put CO_2 limits ahead of the alleviation of poverty. While China is willing to take dramatic measures to reduce actual pollution, they will not accept mandatory limits on CO_2 generation.

Martin Palmer—Pseudo-Science and Pseudo-Religion

The goal of the International Confucian Ecological Alliance (ICEA), according to its Mission Statement, is to address the "increasingly severe ecological crisis and the depletion of natural resources" by merging the "environmental" goals of the British Empire with the ancient Confucian philosophy of the Chinese. The problem they face is that Confucianism at its root is completely incompatible with the anti-scientific, anti-growth, anti-human intentions of Prince Philip's environmentalism.

In fact, when Prince Philip set about to pull the leading world religions into his web in the 1980s and 1990s, he did not even bother trying to recruit the strongly anthropocentric Confucianists, but went directly to the Daoists (Taoists) of China, whose anti-development mysticism, equating man with the beasts and the flora and fauna,—and even the rocks!,—was more in keeping with his aim of depopulation. In 1986, Philip founded the "WWF World Religion and Conservation Network" with his protégé Martin Palmer, and later morphed this into the Alliance of Religions and Conservation (ARC) in a 1995 conference in Windsor Castle.

Prince Philip's servant-man Martin Palmer is in fact a practicing Daoist (as well as a practitioner of many other folk religions). He has translated the basic Daoist texts into English, and has written numerous books on the subject, including "The Elements of Taoism," "Yin and Yang," and "The Book of Reincarnation and the Afterlife." He works closely with the Chinese Daoist Association, which held a conference in London in 2013 in celebration of 20 years of action on ecology. In an essay entitled "Daoism, Confucianism and the Environment" in 2013, soon after the founding of the ICEA, Palmer praised the Daoist principles, including:

• "We should cultivate the way of no-action and let nature be itself;"

• "If the pursuit of development runs counter to the harmony and balance of nature, even if it is of great immediate interest and profit, people should restrain themselves from it. Insatiable human desire will lead to the over-exploitation of natural resources. To be successful is to be on the path of defeat..."

In the same essay, Palmer gloats that the founding of the ICEA "marked the first time a specific Confucian organizational response has emerged to the environmental issues confronting not just China, but the whole world." Although "Confucianism is new to this," wrote Palmer, the creation of his new ICEA satellite group means that Confucianism will "put its energy over the next few years into a sustainable harmonic relationship between humans and nature."

This is Palmer's intention, and that of Prince Philip,—but it is in fact a pathetic attempt to drag Confucianism, and in particular the Confucian revival championed by President Xi Jinping, into the gutter of Daoism and animist folk culture.

In fact, the target is not Confucianism per se, but China itself, and Xi Jinping's "One Belt-One Road," which is taking high speed rail, dams, nuclear power, and similar infrastructure and technology to the developing sector. Palmer openly attacks the "destructive

basis of contemporary Chinese development." In an Oct. 23, 2014 interview with the Pulitzer Center, Palmer said: "How on earth do you stop this juggernaut, thundering forward of industrialization, of pollution, of commercialization and consumerism?"

The Chinese leadership is fully aware of the serious pollution problems facing China, and is taking measures to confront them, but they also know that without further advancement in science and technology, which drives the "juggernaut, thundering forward of industrialization," there will be no solution to either the pollution problem or to the more serious problem of alleviating poverty and sustaining human progress.

In that same interview, Palmer openly promotes the overthrow of the Chinese government. He "predicts" that the "Chinese Communist Party may very well be one of the shorter-lived dynasties in history," because the "relationship between religion and politics will come to a breaking point within the next 20-30 years. In Xinjiang and Tibet, you could argue it already has."

Palmer comes from a long tradition of British intelligence agents working to subvert China. He studied with the late Joseph Needham, who profiled China on behalf of the same circles around Prince Philip. Julian Huxley, who founded the WWF, also worked with Needham in the creation of UNESCO (United Nations Educational, Scientific and Cultural Organization), which was from the beginning an occult-infested British intelligence nest within the UN. Needham also promoted Daoism and denigrated Confucianism, even offering full support to the "Anti-Confucius Campaign" during the nightmare days of the Cultural Revolution in the 1960s and 1970s. (see this author's "The Taoist Hell of Joseph Needham, 1900-1995," *EIR*, vol 22 number 17, April 21, 1995).

Tu Wei Ming—The Conflict in Chinese Antiquity

Prince Philip and Martin Palmer could never achieve the subversion of Confucianism without collaborators within China. Their primary Chinese collaborator, Tu Wei Ming, was born in Kunming, China in 1940, received a PhD from Harvard, and went on to head the Harvard Yenching Institute from 1996-2008. He has become the leading spokesman for a movement known as "New Confucianism," setting up Confucian studies programs in the U.S., Singapore and elsewhere.

But Tu Wei Ming is a dedicated promoter of a very special school within Confucianism, that of Wang Yang

www.daousa.org

The opening ceremony of the U.S. Daoist organization's Universal Consciousness Festival in 2015.

tured in the famous passage from the Daoist Zhuang Zi (399-295 B.C.), who imagines a meeting between a disciple of Confucius and a Daoist peasant who is scooping water with a cup to irrigate his field.

The Confucian says: "If you had a machine here, in a day you could irrigate one hundred times your present area. The labor required is trifling as compared with the work done. Would you not like one?" He describes a well-sweep, whose foot-driven pulley with wooden scoops lifts water from an irrigation ditch into the field. The Daoist peasant denounces the Confucian, insisting that anyone who is cunning with instruments must also have a scheming heart, cannot be pure and incorrupt, and is thus not a fit vehicle for the Dao (the "Way"). "It is not that I do not know of such things," he says, "but I should be ashamed to use them." Thus, Daoism corresponds to the Satanic current in the West which degrades man to an animal, fit only for manual labor and bare subsistence.

Ming (1472-1529), a school which this author has documented extensively. (See "The European 'Enlightenment' & The Middle Kingdom" at http://schillerinstitute.org/fid_91-96/952_middle_kingdom.html). I have shown that it is directly contrary to the thought and mission of Confucius, Mencius, and especially the great Song Dynasty philosopher Zhu Xi (1130-1200).

A brief discussion of the polar opposites represented by these two so-called "neo-Confucian" philosophers, is both necessary and a very valuable exercise in understanding China today, and understanding Tu Wei Ming's role in Prince Philip's subversion of China.

Zhu Xi and his "School of Principle" (Li) in the Song Dynasty restored and advanced the teachings of Confucius (551-479 BC) and Mencius (372-289 BC), the key philosophers of the Confucian school, whose work parallels in time and in concept the Greek philosophers Socrates (470 -399 BC) and Plato (424-348 BC). Confucianism rejected the "all is one" mysticism of Daoism and the Daoist glorification of brute physical labor, by locating the nature of man in the creative power of the mind. The fundamental principle of Confucianism is the concept of "ren," similar to that of "agape" in Christianity: a quality of love for God and Mankind which is located in the unique human capacity for creativity, as being *capax dei,* capable of God.

The Daoist reaction to Confucianism is best cap-

Confucianism was weakened during the first millennium AD, both from Daoist influences and the arrival of Buddhism from India. During the Eleventh and Twelfth Century Song Dynasty, there was a Renaissance of Confucianism known as the "School of Principle," of which Zhu Xi was the leading figure. Zhu Xi explicitly identified the Confucian concept of "ren" as "creativity:" "The mind of Heaven to produce things is ren. In man's endowment he receives this mind from Heaven, and thus he can produce." Zhu Xi argued that the nature of man and of all things in the world, was not located in their physical characteristics, visible to the senses, but rather to an unseen "principle" (Li) of each person or thing, which connected it to the fundamental principle of the universe, with man uniquely capable of acting upon that principle through the human quality of ren, creativity, by "investigating this unseen principle to the utmost" through the creative mind.

This closely parallels the Christian notion of man

created in the living Image of God, *Imago Viva Dei* participating through the creative mind in the unfolding creation of the universe. The great German philosopher, scientist and statesman Gottfried Leibniz (1646-1714), upon receiving translations of Zhu Xi's works from Jesuit missionaries in China, recognized this coherence, and organized support in Europe for cooperation with China based on this principle.

Zhu Xi's ideas became the guiding principles of Chinese education, scholarship, and government service, even in a limited form after the Mongol hordes destroyed the Song Dynasty, but especially under the succeeding Ming Dynasty (1368-1644) and Qing Dynasty (1644-1911). However, a counter-school to Zhu Xi emerged in the late Fifteenth Century under the soldier-scholar Wang Yang Ming (1472-1529), known as the School of Mind. It is this school that our Harvard "New Confucian" Tu Wei Ming follows in arguing that Confucianism is compatible with the British Empire's (and the current Pope's) bestial notion of man as an expendable being polluting "Mother Earth."

I have shown in the cited articles that Wang Yang Ming was essentially a Daoist,—that he rejected man's connection to Heaven through the power of creativity, the capacity to investigate and master the laws of the universe. Wang argued that such investigation was unnecessary since the mind supposedly already contained all that it needed to discern good and evil, and everything that existed in the universe was limited to what could be accessed through sense-perception.

Man is thus reduced to nothing more than a sentient being, as in Daoism and Chan (Zen) Buddhism, unable to change the universe through the discovery of the unseen laws underlying phenomena, which, according to Wang Yang Ming, do not exist.

The character of Wang's Aristotelian rejection of anything other than sense perception, was captured in his own account of a failed experiment he conducted to test Zhu Xi's concept of "principle." He decided to "investigate the principle of something to the utmost," as Zhu Xi had suggested, to discover if its principle actually existed or not. He choose some bamboo in a garden, and sat before the bamboo, gazing at it intensely, attempting to discern its principle, and ignoring the fact that Zhu Xi had demonstrated that the physical appear-

youtube

Prof. Tu Wei Ming of Harvard University heads a school of Confucianism that actually promotes Daoist thinking. Here he gives a talk at the Shaolin Temple Cultural Festival in Los Angeles in October 2013.

ance of something is merely the shadow of its principle, of its true nature. Wang Yang Ming eventually gave up, concluding that since he couldn't see it, the principle of the bamboo didn't exist.

International Confucian Ecological Alliance

So what is the International Confucian Ecological Alliance (ICEA) referenced at the beginning of this article, put together by Prince Philip, Martin Palmer, and Tu Wei Ming, the promoter of Wang Yang Ming's perversion of Confucianism?

The organization describes its mission as countering the "increasingly severe ecological crisis and the depletion of natural resources." Of course, there is no such thing as the "depletion of natural resources," as long as mankind is continuing to discover new principles of the universe and apply them to human development. New technologies redefine the resource base for mankind, as the internal combustion engine transformed oil into a valuable resource, and as fusion power will make the deuterium in seawater a valuable resource.

And, it must be said, the crisis of real pollution (as opposed to the fraud of defining CO_2 as a pollutant, as Obama's Environmental Protection Agency has done) is resolved through new more efficient technologies, not by curtailing industrialization.

Tu Wei Ming issued a "Confucian statement on the

Xinhua/Wang Ping

Hundreds of thousands of deaths from floods like this one in July 2013, have been prevented by China's infrastructure projects, which Prince Philip's Daoists oppose.

Environment" in July 2013, which was read, appropriately, at Prince Philip and Martin Palmer's Alliance of Religions and Conservation (ARC) conference in Norway. There, Tu Wei Ming explicitly denounces anthropocentrism, quoting from his favorite philosopher Wang Yang Ming. Man's true nature, Wang Yang Ming said, "forms one body" not only with the rest of mankind, but also with the animals, with plants, and even with stones. Our true humanity, Wang says, feels pity when a plant is broken and regret when a stone is crushed. "Our humanity forms one body with the tiles and the stones." This is Daoism or worse, but certainly not Confucianism.

Tu Wei Ming concludes: "Humankind has repeatedly abused this beautiful gift [nature] by exploiting it recklessly, ignoring the Confucian notion of balance and harmony."

Not surprisingly, Tu praises Nazi philosopher Martin Heidegger, saying we must "go back to the pre-Socratic period.... It is the obsession with the problem of technology which must be overcome."

Tu Wei Ming's effort to define Confucianism based on the degenerate Wang Yang Ming drives him to quote other ancient thinkers, but here he often contradicts himself, nowhere more blatantly than with Zhang Zai (Chang Tsai, 1020-1077), a leading predecessor of Zhu Xi in the School of Principle. Zhang Zai's "Western In-

scription" was a primary contribution to the Song Renaissance of Confucian thought. Tu Wei Ming quotes from the Western Inscription: "That which fills the universe I regard as my body, and that which directs the universe I consider as my nature."

This clearly anthropocentric statement, uniting man's nature with the director of the universe, as in the Christian notion of Imago Viva Dei, man in the living Image of God, also parallels the biblical mandate for man to "have dominion over nature."

Yet Tu Wei Ming reports that this statement conveys the opposite,—the Daoist notion of the unity of Heaven, Earth, and Humanity,—ignoring Zhang Zai's distinction between mere matter, which makes up the physical universe, including the human body, as opposed to the soul, or the creative power of the mind, which comes from the Creator ("the director").

Tu Wei Ming, like Martin Palmer, has openly expressed his intention to undermine China's phenomenal progress (although he has toned it down a bit since he helped found the Institute for Advanced Humanistic Studies at Peking University and became its Director in 2010). In a 1999 interview in *Philosophy Now*, Tu called on the world to condemn China's human rights violations, and its "aggression" towards Tibet. Then in 2001, in an essay called "Ecological Turn in the New Confucian Humanism: Implications for China and the World," in the journal *Daedalus*, Tu denounced China's "single-minded commitment to progress," and complained that China "has completely turned her back on her indigenous resources for self-realization," and instead embarked on a course of action "detrimental to her soul and her long-term interests," through the "obsession with power and mastery over the environment."

Xi Jinping's Confucian Revival

While Prince Philip's intentions toward China are very clear (after all, China alone has more people than Prince Philip believes should be allowed to exist on the planet as a whole), Xi Jinping and the Chinese leadership are certainly not succumbing to it. The International Confucian Ecological Alliance has nothing to do with the Confucian revival spearheaded by President Xi (other than the intention to subvert it).

The Confucian revival movement under Xi Jinping, both domestically, and internationally though the Confucian Institutes established in cities around the world, is intrinsically integrated with Xi's "Great Project" approach to global development, the New Silk Road concept of building rail, power, water, and other infrastructure projects around the world, collaborating on space exploration and mass scientific education programs. This is a "win-win"

Xinhua/Huang Jingwen

President Xi Jinping addresses an international seminar marking the 2565th anniversary of the birth of Confucius in the Great Hall of the People in September of 2014.

approach based on Confucian "harmony" between man and nature, through mankind's creative improvement of both.

A book recently published in China entitled "Xi Jinping: How to Read Confucius and Other Chinese Classical Thinkers," documents Xi's extensive use of quotes from Confucius, Mencius, and other Chinese philosophers from antiquity and from more modern times. One that stands out is from Sun Yat Sen, the leader of China's republican revolution in 1911 which overthrew the last imperial dynasty and established a Chinese Republic. Xi quoted Sun: "The world moves forward with great vigor and strength. Either you submit to it and prosper, or you resist it at your own peril."

On Our Mission, Commitment, And Method

Here are excerpts from the LaRouche PAC Nationwide Fireside Chat with Lyndon LaRouche on Thursday, October 29, 2015.

Host John Ascher: Good evening, everyone. This is John Ascher welcoming you back to the Fireside Chat with Lyndon LaRouche here on Oct. 29, 2015. I'm going to connect us with Lyndon LaRouche now.

Lyn, do you have any preliminary remarks you would like to make to the folks on the call here this evening?

Lyndon LaRouche: Yes. What we're doing here is not something just to be repeating something or giving a different spin on it. What we're actually involved in, is trying to understand what mankind's real role must be; as otherwise people generally accept what they think is the popular interpretation of the role they should play. And that is often wrong. Because what it does, is it distracts people's attention from what should be the thing they're concerned about. But they don't know that, because in terms of the practice today in public behavior, most people today do not know how to express themselves competently.

They do know how to make a lot of noises and things like that, and stamp their feet and all these kinds of things, but that does not touch [another]. And the best we can do, knowing this, is try to stimulate the people we're discussing with, and hope that they catch on to what we're trying to convey to them as the principle of presenting the arguments which are required for this kind of representation.

Question: Hello, Mr. LaRouche. It is truly an honor to meet you. Pretty much, I have a comment: You know, we are now on the threshold of a new Renaissance; I'm cautiously optimistic about that. We're on the verge of a new Renaissance for all mankind. As a matter of fact, we're probably entering into an era of human consciousness and development, that will prove to be as significant as when man first created fire. We've got a ways to go, and much work to do ...

LaRouche: Yes! [chuckles]

Dante and Beatrice gaze upon the Highest Heaven. An illustration by Gustave Doré of Canto 31 of Dante's Paradiso.

Question continues: ... but we're making the transition, I believe, from simply a planetary species to an intergalactic species. But what is going on here on Earth resonates with the rest of the Universe, and way beyond that, and man is changing geopolitically, economically, morally, culturally, and spiritually, and this profound change in man's way of thinking coincides with the change permeating throughout our Universe.

I just wanted your thoughts on that, sir.

No Understanding of the Meaning of Man

LaRouche: Well, the problem is we don't have a population that is organized in its behavior to meet the challenge of the subject that you just presented. Very few people in the United States have any understanding, any comprehension, of what all this means. That is, what is there about mankind, such that an individual member of mankind knows what,—in a sense,—knows what track mankind must be on? And maybe it's just that person who has that view; but what we want is an understanding of those kinds of reactions, where people are reacting to find the truth about what our mission is in society. We have to develop that capability.

The problem is based on the Twentieth Century, and I'm going to get a little heavy on this thing, because it's very important,—you've raised the question and it has to be dealt with this way. Mankind went down, in a streak of degeneration, with the arrival of Bertrand Russell. We had only one competent scientist in the Twentieth Century. He was a great scientist, but he was the only one who had this quality: Einstein. Einstein was unique.

Since that time, we have people who are trying to struggle, to realize that kind of goal, but they're handicapped by the society which surrounds them, because popular opinion does not recognize the truth,—almost on every situation. Popular opinion in the United States, and I can say fairly, at a good guess, in Europe, too,—that there has been a degeneration in the quality of the human mind, the human mind of individuals, since the beginning of the Twentieth Century. That's a fact.

Now, if you're going to be successful, you have to abandon that now-conventional system. For example, people will use mathematics, and say mathematics is science; well, mathematics is not science; mathematics is a fraud. And Einstein made that point very clear. So what people have done in schools, in their school education, in their other higher education relatively,—most people have been educated to believe in things that are actually stupid or worse than stupid.

So therefore, if you want to get mankind in the kind of direction that you and I have just exchanged, we have to realize that we have to change the way people think, because they've been conditioned, by schools, education schools, by trades, by gossip,—the people of the United States in particular, have generally no competent comprehension of the real meaning of the human species. And that's been a distortion; and the use of mathematics has been the chief source of corruption, which prevents the minds of our citizens from understanding what the reality of economy is, and of society.

So therefore, my problem is, in terms of work, is that I know that most people, even people who are supposedly highly educated, shall we say,—you know, people who are teaching and so forth,—but in general, the so-called authorities in education really are not competent. They have a certain competence. That is, they can take a certain aspect of information and they know how to deal with it; but when it comes to the truth... For example, let's take the case of Kepler, for an example.

Now Kepler was the first person to understand what the meaning of the Solar System was. Now his design was not then perfect. But now we're working on the basis of a Galactic System. And the Galactic System means that everything that we depend upon as mankind, depends on the management of *water*; and the chief source of water for Earth, comes in the Galaxy. It does not come from local sources. The idea is that you have to understand the relationship of Earth in general, on the Kepler system's work and on other things, including the Galactic System. If people don't understand what the Galaxy means,—which very few people, even scientists, know competently...

And so therefore the problem is that we have a mission-orientation to undertake, to educate people who are presumably well-educated, but are actually at the same time incompetent, because the way they approach things is incompetent. And therefore our problem is, if we're going to make sense of what our intention is, we have to think carefully about what the *mis*direction has been, for most people in the Twentieth Century, and now the Twenty-First Century. They become more and more ignorant, more and more in-

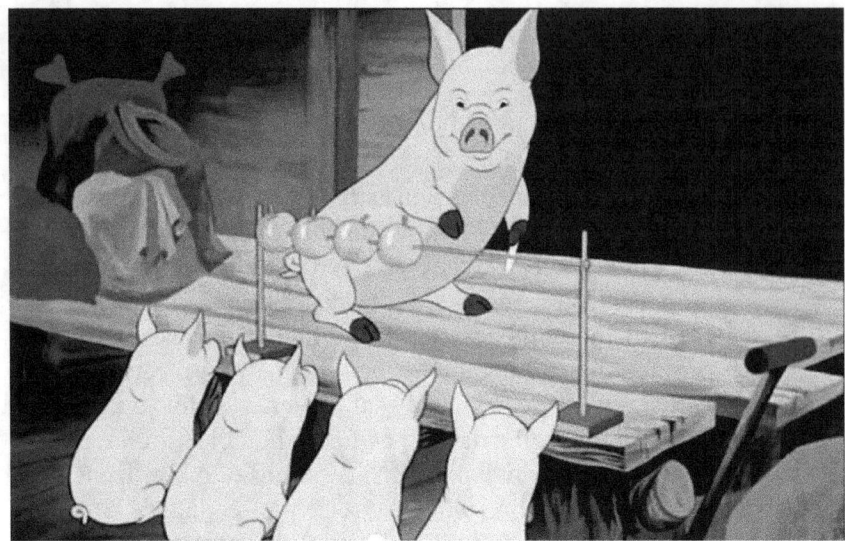

The Twentieth Century world of Bertrand Russell: A snapshot from a British animated film of George Orwell's Animal Farm.

competent. And this is generally true of most of the well-educated people.

What Happened with Bertrand Russell?

So we're at a point now, where we actually have to get at the meat of the area; we have to understand what was wrong about the Twentieth Century, why the Twentieth Century was a betrayal of mankind. And we have to get into what that means, we have to understand it, and we have to apply our understanding, in order to get an access to what we have to do to correct the crazy errors which have gone on in the United States in particular, since the Twentieth Century as a whole, *since* the Twentieth Century now.

So the problem we have, is that it's not enough to argue with people for policies; you have to know what the principle of policy should be. And in the school systems and so forth, very few people understand science, even people who specialize in the subject of science. And what we need is a system of education through discussion, to bring more and more people to understand what the issue is: What was wrong with the Twentieth Century? Why were certain people so evil, so stupid? Because we have to get at that thing, that stupidity is the ruling principle in popular opinion today. We have to free people of that stupidity, otherwise they will go back to the old system, which got them into the mire in the first place.

Question: Hi, Lyn, A— from Los Angeles. Iran sur-

prised me by announcing that apparently they're going to be joining the BRICS pretty soon, so that's a nice development. I was looking at our Silk Road special report: It didn't have much on Iran except a couple of footnotes on the projects we started back in 2000. Now, with the BRICS and the water crisis, and Iran's also facing a major water crisis, I don't know if—it would be cool if we could get some more info on it, if you guys think that would be prudent; I would be more than willing to help if possible. I just wanted to put that out there.

The second thing I was really curious about, Lyn, was that there's people like you and Amelia Boynton Robinson, who really practice the principle of Plato's golden soul. You know, you've been through it. And then, there's people like others that I know, that play video games, and get high, and complain about feminists and immigrants. [LaRouche laughs.] I understand that there's this innate quality of happiness, that Leibnizian happiness and other forms come in with actually doing the right thing; and there's the concept that the good that you do continues to give back; and therefore, your quality of life can be measured in that regard, which is great.

What happens after all that, though, in your opinion? [crosstalk] I would *love* to know!

LaRouche: Well, I say this is the problem. This identifies the problem. First of all, what happened with Bertrand Russell? And Bertrand Russell would say that he was a substitute for Satan. I think that's a fair term of reference. So what we have, is we have a Satanic policy which is a reflection, in particular, of Bertrand Russell's existence. Now, he's dead now, which is something of a blessing, but there's no practical benefit supplied to get rid of him, get rid of his evil.

So the problem is that mankind in general, because of the influence of the Twentieth Century and what is now the extended version of the Twentieth Century today,—the problem is that people don't have an efficient moral view of mankind.

The problem is, and I say this repeatedly at various occasions because it comes up so naturally: Mankind has the ability potentially, because of mankind, to create an arrangement under which living people are actually made to develop in a superior quality of work over their predecessors; that is, mankind is not something devoted simply to living people. Mankind is devoted to the effect of future living people in society, the development of those people with those qualities, in order to move society to have a passion for the development of mankind, a real development. And that does not function today.

And the Twentieth Century became, after Franklin Roosevelt's death and some things related to that,—the United States in particular, as well as Europe, has degenerated in general, degenerated morally and intellectually. You see what's happening in the school system, what's happening in the education system, say in California; the situation there. There is no future for mankind under the policy of the followers of the governor of California; he's a killer, he's an inhuman killer. That is, he acts in violation of the principle of humanity.

And throughout society, evil is spread freely; and what is needed, as the good, as the inspiration, as the purpose to mankind, has a difficult time in making the way ahead.

Question: Hi, this is E— from Delaware. Well, how're you doing?

My Work for President Reagan

LaRouche: Well, I'm old, as you may know, but the good part about it is the fact that I'm still alive and capable of doing things; not as much as I was before physically, but intellectually, I've scrapped a lot of things that I knew before, because I realized they weren't much good for me to use, and I think now I'm operating on that basis. So I'm quite happy with what I'm doing. I'm sometimes dissatisfied, acutely dissatisfied even, by what is *not* being done, which should be done. I think that's a fair summation of what I could say on that subject.

EIRNS

Lyndon LaRouche and his wife Helga touring the Seabrook, N.H. nuclear plant during his 1980 Presidential campaign for the Democratic Party nomination.

Question continues: All right, well, if I may ask a question: You brought up over the last week or two your role in the Reagan Administration, and you've just said a little bit already today. But my question is in regard to this: What is the most important thing that we need to communicate to people today about that previous history, that will enable us to awaken, to move people back to a resistance against this fascist policy? Which not only crushed you, but also crushed the Fusion Energy Foundation which you created, and this was a crime against humanity. And what's the most important thing we need to communicate about that, in the period right now?

LaRouche: Okay, let's take my role in this process. You know, at a certain point in the '70s, I was running for election for President. Now, the time came that I obviously knew that I was not going to be allowed to win that vote.

What happened is that the last two years of that decade, in particular, I was recruited at the suggestion of persons who had been very close to Franklin Roosevelt. And by taking my affinity, personally, to Franklin Roosevelt, who was dead,—and I've had quite a history on Franklin Roosevelt. For example, I was landed in India on the same day that it was known he was dead. And so therefore I made a statement to military people in our military service in Asia; and I said simply that a great man has died, and therefore we have to commit ourselves as people still serving in the military and otherwise,—we had to pick up the thing, because the people who were replacing Franklin Roosevelt were not exactly the best people.

So therefore, I said this is what we have to do. We have to defend what Roosevelt had accomplished because we knew already at that point, even before he died, that the forces of evil, i.e., Wall Street, had regained control over the U.S. Presidency. We had an enemy to defeat.

So on that basis, I gladly accepted the proffer by a veteran of MacArthur and people like him. And so I was talked to, and advised to prepare myself to become a specialist for the incoming Reagan Administration. That occupied the last two years of the '70s, and I came out of that fully trained; and I had people who were scientists who were also fully trained in what they needed to know.

So I became actually the person who set up the core of the Reagan Administration. What happened was when the President, Reagan, was subjected to an assassination attack by a Bush family associate, then he was weakened. And the fact that he was weakened actually weakened my ability to continue my function on his behalf. But I actually laid it out, and it was arranged that way,—I wasn't sneaking it through. It was arranged that I should do that, and provide a program to clean up what had happened with the attempted assassination of a President.

So I played that role. And because of the power I had, the intellectual power, in influence, they said, "Well, this guy's got to go down." And they wanted to set me down. But some people said, "No, we're not going to let him be thrown down; we'll let him go into prison for a while. It's fake, he shouldn't be there, it's a fraud; it's a Bush family fraud." And everything evil that happened to me was a Bush family fraud, up to the present day more or less, until Obama came along.

So therefore, that's what the problem was.

Now, what I'm doing, knowing that we're in an emergency now,—I know what I had known before; I'm an expert in those areas, and even though my age is not recommended, shall we say, I can do it. And that means I *have* to do it; I have to get the job done. I'm not going to do it by myself, but I'm going to be very care-

U.S. Navy/National Archive

General of the Army Douglas MacArthur, Supreme Allied Commander, reading his speech at the Japanese surrender ceremonies, Sept. 2, 1945.

ful, as I am. I don't want people making a mess of the cause for saving the United States from Bushes and from Obama. And that's what my mission is right now.

And since I'm 93 years of age right now,—celebrated that recently,—I think I can say I'm really dedicated to that mission.

Question: Hi, it's C— from Boston.
LaRouche: Your dialect identifies you.

How Can I Be Effective?

Question continues: OK, good. No, it's good,— what you said before, though, was really inspiring. You know, these Fireside Chats are so enlightening and informative. And I guess I called in before, and there's a rally tomorrow in Boston,—I got to make it there. And you know, 9/11 was the event that woke me up when I started to investigate that.

But actually, if I want to be honest, I saw the "JFK" movie by Oliver Stone, and he's come out with a few movies, and back then, I sort of reacted, "How can this be? They didn't teach us this in schools,—you know Oswald, so and so, and so forth." I just want to read this quote, here, and it's really moving to me, and I've been choked up when I watch this. So, it's Jim Garrison (Kevin Costner), and he's talking at the end of the movie. And just bear with me here:

"An American naturalist wrote, a patriot must always be ready to defend his country against its government. I'd hate to be in your shoes today. You have a lot to think about; you've seen much hidden evidence the American public has never seen. Going back to when we were children, I think most of us in this courtroom thought that justice came into

Devoted to the mission: U.S. soldiers marching during World War II.

being automatically, that virtue was its own reward, that good would triumph over evil. But as we get older, we know that this just isn't true. Individual human beings have to create justice, and this is not easy, because the truth often poses a threat to power, and one often has to fight power at great risk to themselves. People like S.M. Harlan, Lee Bowers, Gene Hill, Willy O'Keefe,—they have all taken that risk, they have all come forward.

"I have here some $8,000 in these letters sent to my office from all over the country: quarters, dimes, dollar bills from housewives, plumbers, car salesmen, teachers, invalids; these are people who cannot afford to send money, but do. These are the ones who drive the cabs, who nurse in the hospitals, who see their kids go to Vietnam. Why? Because they care. Because they want to know the truth. Because they want their country back. Because it still belongs to us, as long as the people have the guts to fight for what they believe in. The truth is the most important value we have. Because if the truth does not endure, if the government murders truth, if we cannot respect the hearts of these people, then this is not the country in which I was born, and this is certainly not the country I want to die in."

And that speech,—it just really brings everything into perspective, all the constituents, everybody in La-

Rouche PAC. I mean, they're all patriots. And good will triumph over evil, if we,—and Oliver Stone, his movies, but I went to sleep. And the Iraq war thing. But I just wanted to read that, because I think everybody knows they did something wrong, certainly with Obama, and just going back to JFK and going back before that with Roosevelt. So I just wanted to read that; I don't have a question. But I appreciate you, sir, Mr. LaRouche, for what you've done and what you continue to do. And thanks for taking my call. Take care.

LaRouche: Thank you!

Question: Hello, Mr. LaRouche. Thank you for being on the air this evening. My name is M—, and I'm in San Francisco. I'm a full-time student and I'm 49 years old. How can someone like me be effective,—I don't want to say "fight,"—against this thing that's happening in the world?

LaRouche: Well, the problem in this matter is simply, you get to the point where you realize,—and this happened in military service in World War II, for example. I know of it in World War I, but I wasn't born until after that time. But I know the point was people gave their lives in warfare in great masses. Now if they were lucky, they served under the right people, like MacArthur. MacArthur saved more citizens than were killed, in a sense; and he always tried to win the war with a certain degree of honor, that is, actually doing a good job.

But the people who died as soldiers on the Western Front, for example, and so forth,—they died because they believed, in one way or degree or another,—they honored the fact that they put their lives in jeopardy for the sake of society and for the sake of their nation, and that's very important.

Like a Soldier's Mission in War

Now, I understand that probably better than most people do because I experienced,—I've been able to monitor this kind of thing and how it's happened, because I've been in many parts of the world involved in serious kinds of undertakings. I spent most of my life until recently travelling all over the world on mission-orientations. And I see this; I see the devotion of the citizens of the United States at an earlier period; at a period of the Twentieth Century and after that, as in the period of World War II.

People died. They didn't intend to die. It was not their intention to die,—a few, yes; they got mad and wanted to kill themselves in a sense to prove how brave they were; but the average soldier or person in service did not want that. They knew and regretted; and they would write letters to their family when they were going into combat areas, and they would say, "I'm here. I'm here; I hope I make it, but I'm going to fight this war to deal with this problem." And that kind of thing doesn't exist much any more. And people don't understand it; they've lost it. They've lost that devotion.

But what we can do, and what I do, is you get people who have lost that business, and who understand what this business meant: The human being's life is not the end-all and be-all of a human life. It is what mankind is able to do in society to build society up, to achieve things for mankind,—and by that kind of approach, that kind of devotion, you build a truly good society.

Now they may have made a lot of mistakes; a lot of soldiers in military service made a lot of mistakes. But the overall intention was they were going to serve, they were going to serve the nation; they were going to protect the nation; they were going to deal with evil, get the evil out of the way. And that attitude has been largely lost.

Now we have soldiers who will kill, but they don't have that attitude any more. Oh, there are a few soldiers, a few key soldiers will have that; MacArthur had that idea; others had that idea and followed it. But in general now, we don't have that kind of devotion. And what is that devotion? To realize that your existence is to create a better future for mankind than would have been available otherwise. And therefore, if you get killed in the process of conducting a mission like that, your life has not been wasted, because what you did was important. And mankind benefitted from what you did, and what you lost in the process of doing it.

That conception, that understanding which I and many other people understood, in military service in World War II—I was not really a shooting specialist; I did all kinds of things which weren't very fun, but I was devoted to the mission. And I'm still devoted to the mission.

Question: Good evening, Lyn. This is G— in Minneapolis. Lyn, I've been a follower for more than 30 years, and some of the things that you've said, specifically with respect to creativity and mathematics, literally brought me to tears. I want you to know that; that was a fight that I was having with the University of Minnesota, and nobody seemed to understand.

LaRouche: [chuckles] I know.

Question continues: My question is, if we look at the need for the vitality of an economy, which we had,—sometimes it was overheated, other times it seemed to be running well… We have a situation where we need smart people to participate at the productive level, there is no question of this. They need to be born and they need to be educated. The situation of birth is a critical item; we've aborted 60 million children; we've probably eliminated three or four times that through birth control.

But clearly this damage to the Anglo-Dutch banking system is very deep, and they're trying to recover with things like a tax on carbon emissions and a new tax on health care. But this is finished, and we're going to consider going back to the credit system. How do we think of the vitality of the productive output under the credit system? Will it recover automatically? Or do we need to rethink this, to force it to recover?

LaRouche: Don't take any risk. Make sure that you have an efficient approach to realizing that objective. I

EIRNS/Juliana Jones

"The educational process is also a social process." Here, LaRouche (second from right) discusses with youth at a Schiller Institute cadre school in 2003.

and the whole legacy of Nicholas of Cusa, and what followed from that, you get a very clear sense of what the meaning of life is. It's not just a Catholic doctrine, it's a principle. It's a principle which in and of itself fulfills that role.

Question: This is T—. I'm calling from Virginia. And I'm always inspired and excited to hear these calls, and earlier, Mr. La-Rouche, you were mentioning how to get people's minds focussed on the truth of what's really happening, as well as mankind's mission to leave behind greatness for future generations.

And my question is this: How can I convey these ideas to people? With my generation, that's obviously degenerate,—and I think the biggest problem that I face is there's no real concept of truth being absolute. And I've shared some of these calls on YouTube with people that I know, and they say they can understand it, but I know they can't,—because for one, they don't believe Classical music to be superior, for example. And plus the fact that it took me nearly two years to really get this. So, how can I overcome this hurdle in order that I can be an effective leader?

LaRouche: Well, first of all, you've got to have access to information of a certain type. In other words, the question is, you say, "Well, I've got an idea." You say, I'm going to try to make this idea work, and you say "Well, how do I make this idea work?" I want to accomplish something; how do I do that? And the problem is, you need a system under which people who are working together, actually work on that subject. And work *on* the subject, not *at* the subject, but to win the subject: that is, to actually understand what the measures are that have to be done.

Now, what I do in general on this point,—I'm very fussy about this: that mankind has a creative power,

don't think you—it won't work by your just watching it. You have to make it move, and you have to know what you're doing. And I think when people are well-educated, especially when people are well-educated and are using it for that purpose, it works! It always did work.

The Educational Process is a Social Process

What happens now,—you get the people are so demoralized! Under the reign of the Bushes and Obama, the demoralization of our citizens is a monstrous thing! And that's what the problem is. I mean, we are no longer creating anything worthwhile; there may be something useful being created, but for the most part, everything that's being done is waste.

You have a new Pope. He's not really new. But he's sucked into a Satanic cult, which says "No development of mankind." It's a Satanic cult! And somehow this Pope got sucked into supporting this stuff. I have no idea how; I worked closely with some Popes at a certain point in my life; my wife was also active in that. So I have some sense of what this means, and I can tell you the problem is, it ain't Christianity any more! It's just some kind of a cult.

And whereas when you look at Nicholas of Cusa

which means that, in effect, every human being who comes under the influence of that power of insight, not only *intends* to do something good, but has come to understand the way in which that goodness can be achieved. And therefore the practical question, which is a certain kind of special practical thing,—many people want to do something good, but they don't know how to do it. They say, "Yes, this would be good.—if it would work out." But they don't have any sense of how it would work out. And therefore, the important thing is to inform people, and give them an exposure of how this thing works; how mankind is able to achieve things that mankind had not been able to understand before.

And that's an educational process, and the educational process is also a social process. Because you don't learn things because somebody tells you something, or you say something and use that statement—that does not solve the problem. You have to have an insight into what will actually do the job. And that takes some work.

But then you catch on to it. And the idea is, you need people who are meeting together, who are working together; and in that process you'll find that a group of people can come to an understanding of

A model of Classical education: A Roman mosaic of Plato's Academy in the First Century A.D., in the National Archaeological Museum of Naples.

what they had not fully understood before. They see the errors of assumptions that they made about what they thought was going to be good, and then they realize that was not the right choice; that was not exactly what they should be doing.

But when you get people who are serious about realizing that, and when other people with them are stimulating them to understand what this means, what success means,—you're on the way to the right course.

Ascher: I wanted to see if you have any final comments here, to close our Fireside Chat for this evening?

LaRouche: I think what we have to do is discuss among ourselves,—that is, those of us who have been meeting,—and come up and say, "We are going to organize among ourselves, to do for ourselves what is needed and to lay the laws down which must be applied to save this nation." And I believe that devotion, serious devotion to mission, is the road which has been done in the past time,—is the road to get the American people back into control of their own government.

Ascher: Thank you very much, Lyn, and we'll be back with you next week.

LaRouche: Thank you!

LaRouche's Manhattan Party: Moral Compass for the Nation

by Robert Ingraham

This article was prepared from interviews conducted with numerous leaders of the Manhattan Project.

Nov. 1—Moral Courage. What is it? How does one acquire it? Why is it a singular force with the power to change the future of the nation and the world?

Slightly more than one year ago Lyndon LaRouche initiated a project—the "Manhattan Project"—for the purpose of developing a new leadership for America, a leadership capable of meeting and overcoming the life-and-death crisis we are now facing. LaRouche made clear from the beginning that such leadership could not be found in outpourings of populist rage nor in macho posturing. Rather, what was necessary was an elevation of the souls of a growing force of patriotic volunteers, individuals willing to work on developing the better sides of their nature, to locate their individual identities in the fight for humanity's future.

Although our fight is far from won, it must be reported at this juncture that just such a leadership has not only begun to coalesce in Manhattan, but, even in its still embryonic form, the initiatives undertaken by LaRouche's Manhattan Party are already impacting the political process of the entire nation. Furthermore, it is a force which our enemies are completely unprepared to meet in battle.

The choice of Manhattan should not be a mystery. It was the Manhattan Party of Alexander Hamilton, between 1787 and 1797, which provided the leadership that created the United States of America. From the beginning of the Manhattan Project, Lyndon LaRouche has insisted that the entire effort must be grounded in the Hamilton Principle. In recent months, LaRouche has broadened and deepened the nature of the project to include a leading emphasis on the Choral Principle. These are not two different things. Both are unified in the Conception of Man, what it means to be Human, and LaRouche's message is that all politics is Principle—nothing less. Politics is not about "issues."

In the work of recruitment to the Manhattan Project, this universal concept of humanity has come up again and again in discussions of "immortality," both in terms of the day-to-day political work being done, but more intimately in the music work. And in recent months it has been the choral and related music work which has witnessed the most dramatic effects in the changes in people's self-identities, in "strengthening the souls" of both new recruits and experienced organizers.

EIRNS/Stuart Lewis

Alexander Hamilton, founder of the American Dream. This statue is near the site of his Society for the Establishment of Useful Manufactures near Passaic Falls, New Jersey.

In what follows in this article, we are not presenting "what the LaRouche organization is doing in New York City." This is a briefing on a revolution in progress, one which holds out hope to save this nation at this very late date of corruption and collapse. It is a revolutionary process which needs to be replicated throughout the entirety of the United States.

I. Hamilton's New York

In New York Harbor stands the Statue of Liberty, a manifestation for the entire world that New York City is the gateway to the Beacon of Hope and Temple of Liberty that Alexander Hamilton's New York has represented for more than 200 years. As **Executive Intelligence Review** has demonstrated,[1] Hamilton's New York has always been the headquarters in America's battle against empire, and the concurrent battle to create a nation and a pro-human economic system, based on a recognition of what it means to be a human being, and what should be the governing principles of a human society.

From the time of the Constitutional Convention onward, it was Hamilton who led the fight to free America from the oligarchical feudal heritage of Europe. It was Hamilton who led the nation against the British Empire. And it was Hamilton who was the mortal enemy of the Slave System of Virginia and the South. It was Hamilton who committed the nation to a policy of rapid industrial, technological and scientific development, to the rapid advancement in the productive powers and cognitive skills of the people, and it was this outlook that took root in the American tradition that each generation would be an advance over the last, that children would have better futures than the lives of their parents. It was Hamilton who was the author of the "American Dream."

Hamilton was responsible for the Credit System through which he pursued national economic development. Hamilton, his friends, and his followers were responsible for the creation of modern Manhattan, the building of the Erie Canal, and the creation of the New York public education system, which even in this day, with more than 1.2 million pupils, is the largest in the United States. Progress and Opportunity, that is Hamil-

ton's legacy, and it was continued by people like Gouverneur Morris, Stephen Van Rensselaer, James Fenimore Cooper and others up through the Civil War. And it still exists today.

Hamilton was also the deadly foe of what we today call Wall Street. Despite attempts by neo-cons to claim Hamilton as one of their own, Hamilton hated speculators and financial wheeler-dealers. When people like William Duer tried to get rich off projects such as Hamilton's manufacturing works in Passaic, New Jersey, Hamilton denounced them. He refused to speculate in real estate as many of his friends did. His commitment was to the future, to what was being built, and to make possible a basis for future generations to build more. To advance.

That is Hamilton, and his Principle still lives in the hearts of many New Yorkers. Manhattan is the only place where the revolution initiated by Lyndon LaRouche could begin. It is the point of origin, and it will spread from there.

II. The Choral Principle

During the next seven weeks the LaRouche Manhattan Chorus will stage two public performances of George Frideric Handel's *Messiah*, one in Brooklyn and the second on the upper East Side of Manhattan.

These two concerts, which will include the participation of a growing number of volunteers who have been recruited to the Manhattan Community Chorus, are the latest breakthroughs in an ongoing escalating process stretching back several years, a process intended to evoke from the minds and hearts of New Yorkers higher-order concepts, including concepts involving the idea of culture, the idea of beauty, and the idea of what the human identity is all about.

The decision to found a public community chorus was made because of the recognition that such an uplifting and improvement in the moral character of the people was an indispensable necessity, without which it were impossible to win the fight now confronting us. Throughout 2015, LaRouche organizers have been actively, aggressively recruiting to the Manhattan Chorus. This has included the distribution of a leaflet-invitation, titled *The Classically-Tuned Chorus as a Moral Institution: a Declaration of War on the Stupidity and Banality of Popular "Culture."* We quote here from that leaflet:

---

1. See *Manhattan's Struggle for Human Freedom Against the Slave Power of Virginia*, **EIR**, May 8, 2015.

The NYC Community Chorus performing at the Flatbush-Tompkins Congregational Church on Oct. 25, 2015. The sacred works were performed at the Verdi tuning.

Not only in art, but also in scientific endeavor, shining exceptions aside, humanity has been 'dumbed down' and brutalized in the course of two world wars instigated by a network of degenerate misanthropes known as the British Empire, dead-set on eliminating the majority of humanity and keeping the remainder in a state of largely self-imposed slavery.

It is high time to reverse that course, and open the floodgates of creativity which uniquely define what our Declaration of Independence terms 'the pursuit of Happiness.' And what better and more joyous way to do that, than to build a mighty Chorus of souls dedicated to rediscovering the almost-lost principles of Classical composition embodied in the greatest works of J.S. Bach, of Mozart, of Beethoven, of Schubert, Schumann and Brahms?

The same leaflet begins with a statement proclaiming the role of both Lyndon and Helga LaRouche as the initiators of the Manhattan Chorus project, thus identifying this effort as a political, not "artsy-fartsy," intervention into the New York environment.

The Manhattan Choral project has been a dynamic work-in-progress. Hundreds of New Yorkers have participated in one or more choral sessions. The leaflet quoted above has been distributed on street corner deployments, at rallies, at music schools, posted on Craigslist, and circulated by numerous members of the Manhattan chapter of the LaRouche movement. Recruitment to the chorus and the "political" organizing and interventions have been carried out as one seamless operation. The message has remained constant: "We are creating something better than what exists now. We are determined to recognize the humanity within each of us and to do battle at the highest level for a better future."

There is no easy way to report on the entirety of this effort, so a few stories or anecdotes will have to suffice:

There is the story of one man, the music director of a church, who recently invited leaders of the Manhattan Chorus to participate in a music festival which included choirs from some of the black churches of the city. In particular, he wanted our members to inject Classical music into an event which was otherwise dominated by gospel music. The Manhattan Chorus performed Mozart's *Ave verum corpus*, Bach's *Jesu, meine Freude*, and Hall Johnson's spiritual *When I was sinking down*. This same individual has worked with the Schiller Institute for years in the campaign to return the accepted singing pitch of all of the choruses and choirs in New York to the natural Verdi pitch of C-256. More recently, he has adopted a personal mission to tune down all church pianos in New York to this natural pitch, and he has also undertaken a project to tune his church organ to the same C-256 pitch. When that re-tuning is completed, it will be celebrated by the Manhattan Chorus with a performance of Giuseppe Verdi's *Four Sacred Pieces*.

Another musical conductor was met at a field deployment and signed up to impeach Barack Obama. He then came to one of the Manhattan Chorus rehearsals, bringing with him a young tenor. The tenor left the rehearsal because he claimed to be apolitical and was offended by a poster of Obama with a Hitler mustache. But he was re-contacted, and after further discussion, he came to our next rally at the United Nations and began attending chorus rehearsals regularly. Eventually, this "apolitical" tenor traveled to Washington D.C. as part of a LaRouche-PAC lobbying team to tell Congress to remove Obama from office.

Among the hundreds of people who have participated in the Manhattan Chorus, many of them originally from BRICS nations, there is the classic New York liberal woman, an original cast member from *Hair*, who is provocatively spreading discussion of LaRouche everywhere she goes, particularly in liberal hangouts. There is the political supporter who donated a harpsichord, which is now being played by another supporter/collaborator, who herself has sung in performances of Bach and the Messiah by the Manhattan Chorus. There is the sheet-metal worker who astounded everyone with his performances from Verdi's *Rigoletto*. There is another woman, active in the chorus, whose brother worked on Ronald Reagan's Strategic Defense Initiative.

There is an entire network of professional and semi-professional opera singers who are committed to both the Verdi tuning and to bringing beauty back into the cultural decay of New York. There are the numerous house meetings of singers, conductors, instrumentalists, and political activists which are taking place all the time, meetings which can only be described as an incipient pro-human, pro-beauty resistance movement.

In addition to the brand-new members, a number of singers, music directors, and conductors now participating in this effort are older friends who have "rejoined," having participated in the 1990s in the Schiller Institute's campaign to return all Classical music to the natural human tuning of C-256. Some of them had at-

Dana Carsrud/Schiller Institute

Soprano Rachel Hippert sings Desdemona's aria "The Willow Song" from Giuseppe Verdi's opera Otello, *at the Schiller Institute's Sept. 26, 2015 Musikabend.*

tended Schiller Institute workshops with Carlo Bergonzi and Piero Cappuccilli in New York and Milan, Italy during that earlier period, but fell away either for their own reasons, or due to mistakes that were made by some of the then-leaders of the LaRouche movement. Several of these musicians have expressed their exhilaration at being able to participate again.

These are just a few examples of a much more in-depth complex process, and all of this is sending out a message to New Yorkers: You do not have to be a second-class citizen, either musically or otherwise. You do not have to succumb to the fear and tension which has gripped the city since 9/11. You do not have to accept the Wall Street-directed destruction of the city by the recent string of mayors who have gussied up Midtown Manhattan for the tourists, while the rest of the city has been left to rot. You don't have to accept death and ugliness. There is a pathway out, but it lies not in "protests," but in transforming the souls of citizenry.

There are more than 500 choruses and choirs in New York City, very few of them connected to the professional "music mafia" of the city. The majority are affiliated with churches, and semi-hidden within these networks are many individuals who continue to work day-in and day-out to keep alive a spark of beauty within the city. It is within these extended circles that the efforts of the Manhattan Chorus have begun to spark a response, like an ongoing chemical reaction, linking the fight for musical beauty with the political effort to save humanity.

III. The Manhattan Party in Action—Speaking Truth to Evil

Imagine a hypothetical gathering, where you are with a group of friends, or relatives or co-workers. Normally, such social assemblies are characterized by inoffensive banal "small talk." Would you be willing, in such a milieu, to say "Obama is a murderer," and when people objected, to follow that up by saying, "The President of the United States—our President—murders people in cold blood for pleasure?" Most people, even if they knew such a statement to be true, wouldn't,—unless they were sure that everyone within earshot was of a similar view.

Such cowardice which prevents you from simply stating a moral truth, is the disease that is putrefying both our culture and the souls of our citizens. This is the moral cowardice that afflicts virtually every member of the United States Congress, but it is also the cowardice which overwhelms almost all American citizens. It is the type of cowardice immortalized by the confession of Martin Niemöller,[2] in the words:

> First they came for the Communists, and I did not speak out because I was not a Communist. Then they came for the Socialists and the Trade Unionists, and I did not speak out because I was neither. Then they came for the Jews, and I did not speak out because I was not a Jew. And then they came for me, and there was no one left to speak out for me.

The simple truth is that Obama *is* a murderer, and he must be removed from office. At the same time, Wall Street must be pre-emptively shut down, and the power of the speculative institutions and financial oligarchies eradicated forever.

One year ago Lyndon LaRouche initiated the Manhattan Project. Over the course of the last twelve months, organizers of LaRouche's Manhattan Party have repeatedly made the decision to speak these truths to the citizens of the city, and to intervene uncompro-

misingly against the representatives of Wall Street and the British Empire whenever they attempted to spew their filth in any public venue.

Beginning last year, the LaRouche organization began a series of regular Manhattan Town Meetings, which featured guests such as Helga Zepp-LaRouche, former Attorney General Ramsey Clark, former Congressman Cornelius Gallagher, and many others. In September, following the appearance of Indian Prime Minister Narendra Modi at Madison Square Garden, where he issued the appeal for a new global order based on the future goals of mankind, this effort took on an even deeper character.

These regular Town Hall Meetings were transformed this June 27th, when Lyndon LaRouche began his live Saturday afternoon dialogues with the residents of New York. For the last four months, New Yorkers have had the opportunity to speak directly with LaRouche, ask questions, raise doubts, or say anything that is on their minds. Perhaps the most striking thing about these meetings has been their truthfulness, and it has been out of these honest discussions that a new organization is being built. On Sept. 12, 2015 LaRouche was joined by his wife Helga, Ramsey Clark, and former U.S. Senator Mike Gravel of Alaska, at a special New York City conference, titled "Creating A Peace Paradigm: A New Era For Mankind Where We All Become Truly Human." There the speakers presented the clear choice now facing mankind between death and destruction versus a new Renaissance of human civilization.

In January of this year, the Manhattan Party began a series of political rallies on Wall Street, demanding the impeachment of Obama, the shutdown of Wall Street, and the immediate re-enactment of Franklin Roosevelt's Glass-Steagall policy. These Wall Street rallies have continued on a regular basis, with at least one rally being held every month.

Other rallies have been regularly held at the United Nations, at Federal Hall, at Jamie Dimon's[3] headquarters on Park Avenue, at the offices of the Hongkong and Shanghai Banking Corporation, and many other locations. Organizing squads have regularly deployed throughout Manhattan, including extensively into the Upper West Side, a key neighborhood where a decent-sized chunk of the city's intellectual leadership resides.

---

2. Martin Niemöller was a German Lutheran pastor and theologian, imprisoned in concentration camps from 1937 until his liberation in 1945.

3. Dimon is the chairman, president and chief executive officer of JP Morgan Chase.

EIRNS/Frank Mathis

LaRouche PAC organizing in downtown Manhattan, Oct. 20, 2015.

Also, in addition to the music work described above, both Lincoln Center and Carnegie Hall have been sites for regular organizing and literature distribution, and Manhattan Chorus-sponsored *Musikabends* (German for "music evenings"), have been held once a month. The Manhattan LaRouche Chapter also meets every week, and it has continued to grow in size and power.

In all of these activities, a new membership has come into existence, with new people being recruited through the Saturday dialogues with LaRouche, through the Chorus, or simply off the street organizing. All of these people represent recruits into the battle and a new potential for victory.

On July 13th of this year, LaRouche organizer Daniel Burke confronted Hillary Clinton at the New School in Lower Manhattan, asking her the simple question, "Senator Clinton, will you restore Glass-Steagall?" When Clinton demurred, and then later let it be known through a spokesman that she opposes Glass-Steagall's re-enactment, she forever disqualified herself as a legitimate Presidential aspirant. Since that intervention against Mrs. Clinton, organizers of the LaRouche movement have made a point of confronting and challenging representatives of London and Wall Street wherever they have attempted to speak in public. In recent months more than one hundred such interven-

tions have been carried out. The message has been clear: no longer will murderers, speculators, and thieves be allowed to speak in public unchallenged.

The list of creeps who have been so far confronted is too long to go through, but it includes: Ben Bernanke (former Chairman of the Federal Reserve), Timothy Geithner (former U.S. Treasury Secretary), Lord Adair Turner (former Chairman of the British Financial Services Authority and former vice-chair of Merrill Lynch Europe), and Mervyn King (former Chairman of the Bank of England). These people have been challenged for their murderous policies at public speeches, symposia, book-signings and other venues. In all of these cases, without the presence of the LaRouche organizers, no one else in the audience would have dared stand up to them.

These months of organizing have been a continual self-correcting process. For example, at one event with Ben Bernanke, organizers failed to intervene until the very end of the event, at which point their challenge to Bernanke had little impact. At the next intervention, against the agent of the British Monarchy Lord Adair, a team of organizers repeatedly challenged his lies and murderous intent. Finally, one member demanded that he go back to London and "open a pig farm with David Cameron." This organizer later stated that he had overcome his "fear of authorities" through his work in the Manhattan Chorus,—a chorus he had originally been reluctant to join.

For his part, Lyndon LaRouche has said that the courage of the Manhattan members in publicly challenging these representatives of the British Empire in New York qualifies them as True Statesmen.

IV. Spreading the Revolution

First, a warning. One cannot simply take what the LaRouche organization is doing in Manhattan and "rep-

Astronaut Scott Kelly recently took this photo of New York City from the International Space Station.

licate" it in other parts of the country. Very simply, there is only one Manhattan, and its unique significance exists nowhere else. As Leibniz demonstrated in his arguments against Samuel Clarke, one cannot simply move pieces of the universe around arbitrarily.

Manhattan is the intellectual and cultural capital of the United States. Although most Americans will cringe to hear it, the average Manhattanite is smarter than the average American. There is a reason why Hamilton and his group were based in Manhattan, why Lincoln gave his history-changing Cooper Union speech in Manhattan, why Ulysses Grant is buried in Manhattan, and why, in 1967, Martin Luther King traveled to the Riverside Church in Manhattan to deliver his historic speech breaking with Lyndon Johnson on the Vietnam War. At the same time, Manhattan is also the nesting place of the Wall Street parasites and the financial murderers of the British Empire. In other words Manhattan is a battleground—*the key battleground*—in the fight for the

soul of the nation, just as it has been since the days of Alexander Hamilton.

So, it must be said that there is no simple recipe which one can apply from the Manhattan Project in other locations. Nevertheless, if what has been presented above is sufficiently coherent, it should be clear that the approach to saving humanity, providing hope, awakening moral courage and courageous truthfulness,—which are all facets of the organizing of the Manhattan Party,—are lessons that can be applied everywhere in the pursuit of victory.

We live in a culture in which young people are drowning in bestiality, and where the message to anyone over 50 years old is, "just drop dead; you have nothing to live for, and you are useless to society." It should come as no shock to anyone to see the current dramatic increase in suicides among the Baby Boomer population. Everywhere in the country there is an omnipresent sense of foreboding, nervousness, and fear of the future. *But there is a way out!* In particular, the continuing work and breakthroughs of the Manhattan Choral program give a glimpse of that way. Not music to be "arty," like some over-dressed matron at the gala opening of the opera season. Rather, the reawakening and strengthening of the human soul, of that which differentiates us from beasts. That is the pathway to recruitment and to victory.

There is no recipe. There is simply the **desire in our hearts** to work on it, to improve it. This is not a movement that one can "control," nor should one try to. There is no Comintern party line. It is rather a process of moral liberation. And from moral liberation comes courage.

A Resolution To Defend the Lives of Billions of People:

We Say NO to the Paris COP21 CO_2 Reduction Scheme

Nov. 2 (EIRNS)—The following resolution was released today by Schiller Institute, with the intention of rapidly collecting signatures from qualified professionals, political leaders, and ordinary citizens internationally.

The conditions of life for billions of people depend upon rejecting the agenda being presented at the 2015 United Nations Climate Change Conference to be held in Paris this December. The COP21 Paris initiative to adopt a legally binding agreement to reduce CO_2 emissions must be rejected on two grounds: the scientific reality that mankind's activity is not going to cause catastrophic climate change, and the very real, lethal consequences of the CO_2 reduction programs being demanded.

There is no legitimate basis for having the COP21 conference. Put an end to this now!

Despite the climate-change narrative being presented by an extremely well-funded, top-down propaganda campaign, there is an immense amount of solid scientific evidence which clearly contradicts and/or refutes the claims of coming catastrophic climate change caused by human emissions of greenhouse gases. For example, satellite measurements have shown that there has been no average rise in global temperatures for over 18 years, despite the fact that human greenhouse gas emissions have been increasing at an accelerating rate. This underscores the reality that the climate simply does not respond to CO_2 levels in the way claimed by climate alarmists; said otherwise, the Earth's climate system is not highly sensitive to changes in atmospheric CO_2 concentrations.

Because many climate models are using these false assumptions of high climate sensitivity to CO_2, the predictions of these climate models have been consistently wrong, and with each year they are diverging further from reality. The gradual changes in the climate that have occurred over the recent decades, and the gradual changes which will continue to occur in the future, are not and will not be a cause for alarm. Most of these changes are natural, and any impact mankind may have would be relatively minor. A healthy and growing world economy will be able to adapt to these changes.

We must also recognize that CO_2 is not a pollutant—it is an essential part of the biosphere. Because the present atmospheric CO_2 levels are well below the optimum for plant growth, human-caused increases in CO_2 concentrations are already contributing to increases in agricultural productivity and natural plant growth—creating a measurably greener planet.

But the Paris 2015 summit is not only about nations potentially wasting time and resources on a phantom problem existing only inside computer models—the ugly reality is that the CO_2 reduction programs being proposed would increase poverty, lower living conditions, and accelerate death rates around the world. The world simply cannot support a growing population with improving conditions of life using only solar, wind, and other forms of so-called "green" energy.

More to the point, this scheme is being intensely promoted by modern followers of the population reduction ideology popularized by Thomas Malthus. Organizations such as the World Wide Fund for Nature have repeatedly declared that current human population is billions of individuals beyond the Earth's "carrying capacity," and must therefore be reduced by some billions of people. The present push for a CO_2 reduction program is deeply rooted in this Malthusian ideological motivation. But Malthus was wrong in the Eighteenth Century, and his followers are wrong today.

Energy-intensive scientific, technological, and economic growth is essential to human existence. This can be measured by transitions to higher levels of energy flux-density, per capita and per area. Such progress, growth, and development is a universal right, and CO_2 emissions are presently a vital part of that process for the overwhelming majority of the world's population. The adoption of a legally binding CO_2 reduction scheme at the COP21 conference in Paris will condemn billions of people to a lower quality of life, with higher death rates, greater poverty, and no ability to exercise their inherent human right to participate in the creation of a better future for society as a whole.

This is deeply immoral.

For these reasons the CO_2 reduction scheme of the COP21 conference in Paris must be rejected.

Shut Down Wall Street Now, Or Face a Killer, Chain-Reaction Crash

Nov. 1—Restoring the Glass-Steagall Act, immediately, was the focus of a powerful intervention into a New York City Democratic Party public event Sunday where local Democratic officials tried to represent various Presidential candidates, but were forced by the audience to measure those candidates against the standard of bringing back Glass-Steagall and breaking up the Wall Street banks. Representatives of LaRouche PAC started the intervention, and then were joined by many others asking, "Will you restore Glass-Steagall, and will you do it now?"

The LaRouche PAC activists also demanded action to remove the murderer Obama from the Presidency for his crimes of war.

The matter was posed again by Lyndon LaRouche later that day:

If we don't close down Wall Street, we're going to see a crash like never before. Americans and Europeans aren't just losing wages, losing jobs. Don't buy the Wall Street "forecasts of options" for what's now happening. We're talking about a sudden, chain-reaction collapse, unless we intervene to shut down the Wall Street institutions.

And this one will be a killer—the economic collapse is accelerating and condemning Americans to death. In Europe, it's as bad, or worse. The most conspicuous feature of the trans-Atlantic system right now, is the death rates among children.

But the real crisis, he emphasized, is the loss of intelligence among the Congress and the people about what must be done fast, and the replacement of intelligence by cowardice about doing it.

The requirement is not simply to shut down Wall Street and its speculative frauds. It is to *remove it* from the U.S. economy and *replace it* with a buffer of new national credit to sustain productivity, employment, and people.

We can solve this, as LaRouche emphasizes, with the methods of President Franklin Roosevelt. But first, take Wall Street off the table. Shut down the fake economy before its chain-reaction explosion. That means starting with Glass-Steagall restoration immediately. Then, build the real economy.

This does not wait on selecting a new President. It has to be done now, by the people and their representatives, or they will lose everything *before* they get to choose a new Presidency.

Shut down the claims of Wall Street institutions, before they kill us.